THE C.A.L.M APPROACH TO BABY SLEEP

A KIND AND GENTLE STEP BY STEP GUIDE TO HELP YOUR BABY SLEEP WELL

HANNAH LOVE

authors
AND CO.

ISBN13: 978-1-915771-53-7

INTRODUCING THE...

Consistent
Achievable
Loving
Manageable Approach to Baby Sleep

A kind and gentle step by step guide to help your baby sleep well.

Hannah Love DipHe (Nursing) RN (Children) NMC DipION

QR code to Sleep Well Hub.

Please scan this QR code to access your Sleep Well Hub. You will find useful resources, videos, downloads and even weaning recipes to help you on your sleep well journey.

CONTENTS

To my three babies… Oliver, Ella and Henry.

ACKNOWLEDGEMENTS

Thank you to all the families who have put their trust in me to help them with their babies over the years, and from whom I have learnt so much.

A massive shout-out to all my friends. Thank you for always ensuring I keep a healthy balance between work and play.

To my beautiful mum, Claire, who not only showed me how to be an amazing mummy, but how powerful a career helping others can be. I am super proud to follow in your footsteps and help others every day.

To my wonderful dad, Robin, for your support, wealth of knowledge, music, parties, holidays and patience.

Jessamy, my sister and my best friend, thank you for always being close by my side and keeping me topped up with (lots of) food, wine, fun, love, laughter and hugs.

To my children, Oliver, Ella and Henry, for your understanding and patience when Mummy is working and helping other babies. You have all taught me so much more than you could ever know and you make being a mummy easy and fun. Keep being your amazing, completely individual selves. I am super proud of all of you. You are my sunshine.

Finally, to my husband, Daryl, best daddy to our babies, business partner, and biggest support. We are a perfect team, and I couldn't imagine this journey without you by my side. I love you.

Finally, to all the babies who need to learn to sleep well…

FROM ONE MUMMY TO ANOTHER

I honestly thought I would breeze into motherhood. I'd been practising this job for over fifteen years, been in sole care of over twenty-five babies, and spent weeks sleeping overnight with newborns in the same room as me. I was a trained paediatric nurse and here I was feeling far from confident. An alien in my own world.

I don't think anyone can prepare you for those first few days with your baby. Maybe that's why no one tells you how it may feel and everyone focuses on the joy and moments of pure love. No one tells you you'll cry because your partner shaves off his beard. I think my words were, "How can you do that when everything else is changing?" Nobody says you'll break down and shout, "Why on earth do you need to mow the lawn right now?" when all your husband needs is twenty minutes away from his hormone-imbalanced, sleep-deprived wife.

Those first few days do pass quickly, and you absolutely look back with fond memories. I don't have a magic wand to rid your body of hormones or ensure you never have a poor night's sleep but I can offer solutions to the constant questioning of what you're doing, the anxiety parenthood brings, and the exhaustion that goes hand in hand with a new baby.

This book will show you how to teach your baby to sleep well. So many things melt away when exhaustion is eased. When you can sleep the anxiety is turned into excitement, the questions become solutions, and you are able to enjoy all those precious moments with your baby.

HOW TO BEST USE YOUR SLEEP WELL BOOK

Although intended as a book to work through from chapter to chapter, and you should definitely proceed through the programme in this way, you may sometimes need specific advice on a certain topic - for example, coughs and colds if your baby becomes poorly. In that case, you might use the points of reference to those pages.

The programme is split into six modules. The first four complete the sleep training for your baby. By the time you have completed module four your baby should be sleeping well.

Modules five and six are all about moving forward with your baby sleeping well. You will also find troubleshooting and extra information to complement the training. If your baby starts teething during the process, for example, please refer to the teething advice in module six; if you go away on holiday during the programme there is advice about that too.

Don't put the book away once you have completed the programme. Refer back to it when you need to.

Finally, please remember to follow the QR code to your Sleep Well Hub. It will be updated regularly to complement this book and support you on your sleep well journey.

Hannah Love

INTRODUCTION: A BETTER APPROACH TO BABY SLEEP

TRYING EVERYTHING

When I first started helping babies sleep well in 2004, there was very little help or information on baby sleep. I was working privately as a nutritional therapist, and as a paediatric nurse in Accident and Emergency, as well as delivering first aid and weaning classes. As soon as any parent found out I had previously been a nanny and maternity nurse, the conversation always came around to sleep. Parents were exhausted, the lack of information left them with so many questions unanswered, and the only go-to for help was their Health Visitor, who usually only offered advice on how to do controlled crying, something the parents who approached me wanted to avoid.

Fast-forward nearly two decades and times have changed massively: there is almost too much information out there.

You find Facebook communities, thousands of sleep specialists, Instagram reels and accounts, books, not to mention other parents' openness about their baby's sleep and being more than happy to offer their advice. This surfeit of information often leads to what I describe as the 'try everything' approach to sleep.

Consider this scenario:

You decide your sleep situation isn't working for you. You are exhausted, don't have any evenings, can't get everything done and you dream of someone else being able to put baby to sleep. You need to move forward from rocking or feeding your baby to sleep.

What do you do?

You 'try everything' to achieve this; you are desperate. You start with a little shush or pat in the cot. That doesn't work so you do a little pick up/put down. That doesn't work either so you resort to bouncing and patting or walking around. As a last attempt to salvage the situation you try a little 'cry it out' but you can't stand this for long so you end up picking baby up and resorting to feeding or rocking. Both of you are crying, you feel like a failure, and you feel you've just made the whole situation a thousand times worse.

This 'try everything' approach never works. The most important things for any sleep programme to work are the three Cs: being Consistent, Calm and Confident. By swapping and changing, getting upset and not sticking to one thing you are being inconsistent, panicked, and nervous. Exactly the opposite of what your baby needs you to be to learn something new.

Over the last twenty years I have helped thousands of families sleep well with my knowledge, training, and my kind and gentle approach. My method has become so popular that I've moved from helping one-to-one to teaching courses to hundreds of parents in one go. I am so confident I can help any baby that my one-to-one programme has a money back guarantee, something I have never had to honour in the fifteen-plus years I have offered it. Every single parent who has reached the end of the programme and followed my advice has had a baby sleeping independently.

You have already taken the most difficult step: that of choosing the approach that resonates with you. My CALM (Consistent, Achievable, Loving and Manageable®) steps in these pages will guide you through removing the sleep habits you and your baby have formed, and get you both sleeping. No more going to bed with your baby, no more evenings of battling to get your baby to sleep, no more dreading what the night will hold. At the end of this process, you will be putting your baby into their cot when they are tired, saying goodnight and walking out of the room. Even better your baby will be better at sleeping anywhere, no more being tied to the house. You will have the time to get things done and have the energy to do them. You might even be able to enjoy an evening out while a babysitter puts them to bed, or the confidence to take them with you.

You are probably thinking, like many before you, that your baby will be the only one it doesn't work for, the *one* family my approach fails with. In nearly every Trustpilot review and in many testimonials parents write how they felt it wouldn't work for them, followed up by sentences like:

> "Wow, wow, wow. Hannah's course was incredible, so kind and gentle. I never left my little boy's side until I knew he could fall asleep independently."

> "I have gone from feeding to sleep, contact naps, co-sleeping and multiple wakes during the night to putting her into her cot and walking out of the room and she sleeps all night."

> "…it totally changed my life. I was so confident in Hannah I never felt uncomfortable at all. Wish I had known about Hannah sooner, and hopefully if we are blessed with another baby I can follow her advice earlier on. Thanks, Hannah."

You could soon be in the position to write one of these reviews. It might seem a distant dream right now, but you will get there.

THE CALM APPROACH TO SLEEP

The CALM (Consistent, Achievable, Loving and Manageable®) approach gives you the steps to follow to achieve your baby sleeping well.

C gives you a *consistent* approach, one you can all follow as a family. A ensures this consistent approach is *achievable.* You can do things in small steps. L promises a *loving* experience. You can support and comfort your baby… which ensures it is *manageable* for you: the M in CALM.

CALM guides you from where you are now with your baby's sleep, to your baby sleeping on their own and independently settling to sleep, whether that be in their cot or on the go. You practise during your baby's day time first when it's much easier to do new things. You will discover how to get a more predictable day and ensure your little one feeds and eats well. You will also learn about sleep triggers and find a consistent way to allow anyone to settle your baby to sleep.

Once the day time works for you, you'll be able to gradually reduce night-time milk feeds and address overnight wakes, using the skills you and your baby have practised in the day time.

Finally, we start the actual sleep training. This tracks several stages to get baby sleeping independently. There will be *no* leaving baby to cry. You can take this as slowly as you feel comfortable with, each stage moving closer to the endpoint of baby sleeping on their own.

Before we start, I ask one thing of you... to forget what you have previously learnt and to put your faith in me and my approach to baby sleep. If you do that, by the end of this book you and your baby will be sleeping well.

Even more importantly, you'll have the confidence to create more experiences and time together as a family. With less exhaustion and anxiety, you'll enjoy taking them out for the day, the evening, or away on holiday - as you know they will sleep. Through doing the program you'll be able to relax and have fun, as you know they can adapt and it will all be OK.

If at any point you do feel you need more support, you can access this through your Sleep Well Hub.

BREAKING HABITS

Bringing your first baby home from hospital and the few weeks that follow it are overwhelming for all.

I have never met a parent who doesn't feel anxiety, a feeling of muddling through or of doing their best to help and comfort their new baby. One thing is for sure: it's rarely a walk in the park. Babies absolutely do not 'sleep like a baby.'

Parents often, and understandably, fall into habits such as contact napping, cuddling to sleep, feeding to sleep and co-sleeping. Many don't plan it to happen this way: their pre-baby images of baby sleeping in their new Moses basket go out the window and habits form from necessity, exhaustion, and survival.

I never see my job as telling parents how they should look after their baby. Many parents love to contact nap when baby is small and co-sleeping can work well for a period of time for a number of families. But this can't last forever. I am here to offer a solution when you would like to move forward.

Sleep training has a terrible reputation and most parents dread it. It is often associated with leaving babies to cry it out, abandonment, and not meeting their needs. It doesn't need to be like that. The sleep training you learn here simply fast forwards what is often a natural progression with your baby's sleep. Also, if you follow my three key principles (the 3 Cs of *calm*, *consistent* and *confident*) you can have a baby that sleeps well and a loving and bonding experience for both of you.

YOUR BABY CAN SLEEP

Your baby can sleep; they already do sleep: they sleep how you taught them to sleep. Whether that's with feeding, rocking, bouncing, contact napping, in the pram, or a more elaborate way such as standing under the extractor fan while daddy hoovers and mum bounces at one bounce a second while patting their bottom and singing *Twinkle, Twinkle* (this is an actual scenario I've come across)… your baby can sleep.

Babies are naturally restless sleepers. They must wake regularly, and they spend much of their sleep in active, light sleep. Just because they wake lots, move around, fidget, and open and close their eyes, this doesn't mean they don't sleep well. This way of sleeping regulates oxygen levels and protects them against SIDS (Sudden Infant Death Syndrome). It is important.

I'm sure it doesn't come as a surprise: a baby's sleep is completely incompatible with an adult's. We prefer to go into nice long, deep sleep cycles. Waking many times a night is exhausting for us – herein lies the reason your baby wakes up ready to start the day while you need matchsticks to keep your eyes open until the coffee has kicked in!

These two graphs perfectly illustrate the difference between your sleep and your baby's sleep. Babies dip in and out of two sleep cycles – deep and light sleep – whereas adults have much longer sleep cycles. We are not programmed to wake up many times a night but for your baby it is essential.

Typical Baby Sleep

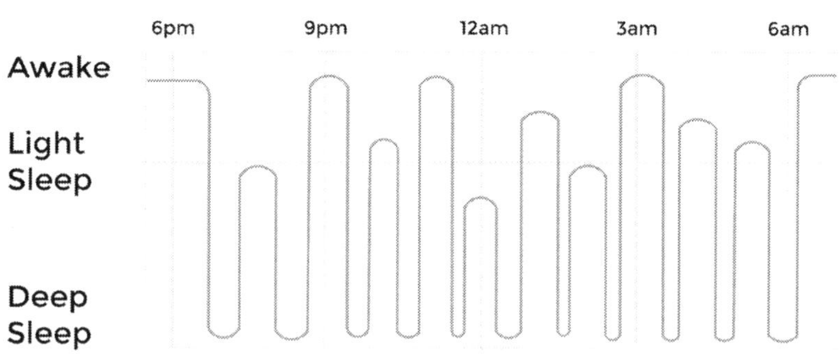

Typical Adult Sleep Pattern

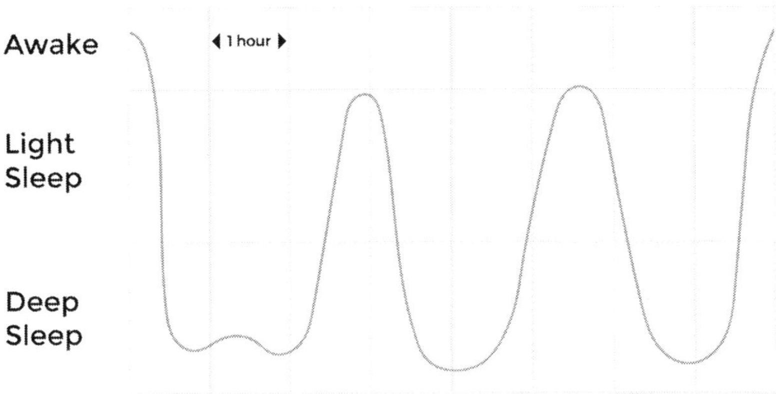

If your baby relies on anything to go to sleep (rocking, feeding, bouncing, etc.), this is what they will need to go back to sleep after every overnight wake, which as the chart shows, is a lot of times each night.

THE FOUR-MONTH SLEEP REGRESSION

In the first few months after birth, if you have a way of getting your baby to go to sleep then most will stay asleep even if transferred elsewhere, unless they are uncomfortable or there's something wrong.

But once they hit four or five months, your baby becomes more aware. This is a beautiful time as they start to laugh at your repetitive actions, recognise you from others, and are happy when you return to them. It also means they start to realise and remember when things change or are missing.

The psychological term for this is 'object permanence' and was discovered by a Swiss psychologist called Piaget. In this developmental stage your baby is now aware of missing objects and changes in a situation. If they go to sleep in your arms but wake up somewhere else, they realise and remember that they have been moved.

Imagine going to sleep in your nice warm bed, and someone taking you out into the garden while you sleep. This happens to your baby each time they wake overnight, having been moved. Babies who can't self-settle are likely to wake more often overnight, take shorter naps, wake on transfer to the cot, want to contact nap, wake early in the morning and need more overnight feeds. Teaching your baby to self-settle to sleep can address all these issues.

WHAT CAN HAPPEN WHEN BABIES CAN'T SELF-SETTLE?

- Wake more often as they get older
- Shorter naps
- Waking on transfer to the cot (even if you lower them like a bomb ready to explode!)
- Only able to contact nap
- Wanting to sleep on you and not in their cot
- Early morning wakes
- Increase in overnight milk feeds
- Distracted daytime feeds or not weaning onto solids well; fussy with food

- False starts in the evening and multiple night wakes

The aim of sleep training is not to get your baby to sleep through. The aim is to teach your baby to sleep independently; to self-settle to sleep so they can carry this skill throughout the whole twenty-four hours. This means they will be able to go to sleep in their cot, not need transferring, not need the overnight feeds to re-settle, and re-settle if they wake in the evening or early morning, therefore addressing all the above common sleep issues.

THERE IS NEVER ANY NEED TO LEAVE YOUR BABY TO 'CRY IT OUT'

Controlled crying, Cry It Out (CIO), Ferber, timed crying, and supported intervals are all methods of getting a baby to sleep independently. There is no 'training' involved and definitely no support. When I see these kinds of instructions being given to parents, I completely understand why sleep training has a terrible name.

There is never any need to leave a baby on their own to cry to teach them to sleep well. You will be there with your baby, supporting them, helping them, teaching them to sleep well. At each stage you'll do a little less and they will do a little more until they are able to sleep on their own.

At the end of the process, your baby will still wake up as many times a night as they are now; the difference is they will be able to get themselves back to sleep without you needing to help them. It is a win-win: you both get the sleep you need and wake up feeling refreshed.

ACCELERATING A NATURAL SLEEP PROGRESSION

When parents contact me for help, their present sleep situation is often dictated by the age of their baby. A small baby's parents are more likely to be standing up or walking around to comfort baby, or feeding to sleep. Once baby reaches around six months, they get too big to be constantly walked around and so parents are usually sitting down, maybe in a rocking chair, on the end of the bed or using a gym ball.

A baby reaches another milestone at around twelve months. A small toddler becomes too big to sit with and bouncing on a gym ball becomes tricky so parents move to settling them to sleep by lying down with them.

These sleep progressions aren't dictated by the baby's mental development. The baby doesn't suddenly think, 'I am now ok to lie down and go to sleep.' The progressions are dictated by the parent's physical need for change. The reason the change works is because subconsciously you apply the three Cs. You can't physically stand with your six-month-old baby so you calmly, confidently and consistently change to sitting down. Your baby adapts.

Similarly, at twelve months you no longer fit in the rocking chair. You move to the bed. You're calm, consistent and confident with the change; your baby picks up on this, see you are ok with the change, and they adapt.

If you try to change before this point – perhaps you try sitting when baby is four months because you feel tired – you don't apply the three Cs. You give it a go, baby cries, and you panic. You know you can stand and so you do. You aren't calm, you are far from consistent, and your confidence is lacking.

This is to be expected. What parent doesn't want to help their baby? What parent doesn't want to calm and reassure their baby when they are upset? But this need to help is the reason most sleep training attempts fail. Doing more never results in your baby learning to sleep independently. Being inconsistent never results in you moving forward with your baby's sleep.

By using the CALM approach you will be Consistent with the change, you will use the Achievable steps, and it will be a Loving process: this will make it Manageable for you and your baby. You will be there to guide and support your baby through the small steps to get them sleeping well and independently. You will show them it's ok… and it will be ok.

FILTER OUT THE CRAP

Too much knowledge will *not* help your baby sleep well.

You have bought the books, joined the parenting communities, followed fifty people on Instagram, are on mums' in baby groups, are visiting the health visitor (if you can get an appointment), and have bought the T-shirt. You know all about wake windows, the average sleep cycle for each age, circadian rhythms and have even examined poo pictures.

When I started helping families sleep well in 2007 very little information about baby sleep was out there. Nothing came up on Google and the only person you could really go to was your health visitor. This made getting help for sleep difficult, but the advantage was that baby sleep was far less confusing.

I am sure this is the reason babies 'used to sleep better than they do now'. (I expect you've been told so by older relatives!) The lack of baby sleep advice meant parents were more consistent in their approach. With only one or two sources of advice they didn't fall into the 'try everything' approach.

For this programme to work you need to use my approach alone, consistently. It won't work if you try to add in other things you've read. You need to forget everything you've read or been told before. Unfollow the Instagram pages. Focus on this one method.

SLEEP MYTHS

Let's debunk some of the many myths surrounding baby sleep that often leave parents conflicted. The struggle of parents I help one-to-one is always due to something they have previously read that has caused them to worry.

"Small babies are not able to learn to settle to sleep by themselves."

A baby of any age can learn how to sleep independently; this can be even encouraged from birth. I used to look after the smallest of babies in neonatal intensive care. We rarely had the time to rock, cuddle or feed the babies to sleep. Each one of them had the skill of sleeping independently. Even once they had 'graduated' from the incubators to the nursery, each one of those tiny babies was able to get to sleep on their own. If they can learn this skill so can your baby.

"Babies don't learn bad habits."

You've all seen the posts: "Cuddling, feeding, and rocking aren't bad habits; they are natural and your baby needs them." Of course, these are natural and if you choose to keep your baby in a sling or to feed them to sleep and back to sleep, that's fine: they aren't bad habits *for you*. But if these things don't work for you, they are habits you'll want to break. Like any habit, with consistency, they can be addressed and reversed, and new habits installed.

"I will need to sleep train my baby over and over again."

Once your baby can sleep independently, they have this skill for life. Regressions may happen and your baby may need reminding, but you won't have to sleep train again.

“You shouldn’t sleep train babies with medical issues.”

I work with lots of babies with reflux, CMPI/CMPA, colic, prematurity, poor weight gain, or cerebral palsy. There are more considerations to make for babies with medical issues but they absolutely can be worked with. *All* babies and parents benefit when they get more sleep. I have added some extra information on this in module six.

“You can sleep train your baby with a ‘no-cry’ solution.”

There is no such thing as a no-cry baby, let alone a no-cry sleep solution. Aiming for your baby to never cry is setting yourself up to fail and all change in babies involves crying. What I promise is that you never need to leave your baby to cry on their own – you may comfort and support them at each stage and remain with them through the training until they can sleep on their own.

“Sleep training will mean I’m tied to the house and not able to do anything.”

Not at all! Please be assured that your baby can fit into your chosen lifestyle. Teaching your baby to sleep well does not need to involve putting your life on hold or being tied to the house. Instead, it means empowering you with the confidence to live and enjoy life, with an adaptable baby who will sleep well – anywhere.

“Sleep training will damage my baby.”

This myth is the biggest of them all. Every single baby and parent is happier once they are sleeping well. There is some evidence that controlled or excessive crying can raise cortisol levels but there is absolutely no evidence that gentle sleep training raises cortisol levels or damages babies.

Perhaps you have read that a baby feels abandoned when you walk out or that sleep is developmental. Forget about all those worrying things you have read. Instead, over the coming chapters, follow each of the six modules of the tried and tested CALM sleep programme that has helped one-to-one clients since 2007 and thousands more in group programmes since 2021.

The first four modules support you to get your baby sleeping well and independently. Modules five and six ensure you have all the tools to stay on track with your baby sleeping beautifully.

INTRODUCING

The…

Consistent

Achievable

Loving

Manageable Approach to Baby Sleep

A kind and gentle step by step guide to help your baby sleep well.

The CALM sleep programme is gradual, delivered through six key modules:

- Module 1 **Preparation**
- Module 2 **Daytime changes**

- Module 3 **Overnight changes**
- Module 4 **Sleep training**
- Module 5 **Finishing touches**
- Module 6 **Moving forward with your baby sleeping well**

MODULE ONE: PREPARATION… FOR YOU AND YOUR BABY

Any big change requires preparation, and sleep training is a big change for both of you. You wouldn't wake up one morning and decide, "I'll move today," you would plan, book the removals van, pack your house into boxes, label them by room, and this would ensure the house move works.

Apply the same principles of preparation to *this* big change to make it run smoothly. This important stage will take a day or two and will have a beneficial effect. The change will be so much easier. Don't be tempted to skip it.

WHY PREPARATION IS SO IMPORTANT FOR *YOU*

This process is always much harder for the parent than the baby. I have witnessed over and over how easily babies adapt if the parents are confident. It is always the parent's confidence in the changes that dictates how smoothly the process goes.

The biggest reason a sleep programme doesn't work is because the parent can't or won't adapt to the change. Sometimes this is temporary – they just need a little encouragement to get back on track or a reminder of why they are here. Occasionally the parent was never on board with the process, their heart wasn't in it, and this shows with the implementation of the advice. You are teaching your baby this new skill. It is a change for both of you. If you want your baby to adapt, you must be open to this.

YOUR REASONS FOR BEING HERE

Make sure you are here for the right reasons so that when things get hard you can return to those reasons as reminders of why you started this process. Write down three reasons why you need or want change for you and your baby.

Here are some good examples:

- I need my evenings back. I spend all evening upstairs trying to settle my baby.
- I am exhausted and can't function in the day time any more.
- I need to move forward from contact napping so I can get things done.
- I want my baby to sleep in their cot so I can have time with my toddler.

- I want to feel confident taking my baby camping.

You will notice these are mainly 'you' focused, and that is fine. Never feel guilty about wanting to change your baby's sleep situation for your own good. Dr Anna Butcher, a counselling psychologist, emphasises that taking care of yourself is vital when taking care of your baby, and reassures parents that making changes to their baby's sleep situation is supportive of the baby, of you, and of the whole family. I have worked closely with Dr Anna since 2015, when I helped her baby sleep well. She quotes Donald Winnicott, a well-known psychoanalyst and paediatrician, who said;

> "There is no such thing as a baby, there is a baby and someone."
>
> — DONALD WINNICOTT

Winnicott meant that wherever there is a baby, there is always another person, a parent or a carer providing care for the baby. Essentially the baby exists as part of a unit with another person. If you get a chance to listen to any of Anna's talks, I recommend them; they are so reassuring.

Other reasons for being here could be baby related:

- My baby is grumpy all the time and needs more sleep.

- My baby is fighting sleep; I need to teach them a way of going to sleep.
- My baby isn't weaning well because they feed all night; I want to teach them to enjoy food as well as sleep.
- My baby feeding all night aggravates their reflux; I need to help them settle without milk.

It is fine to have a mix of 'you' and 'baby' reasons. This process helps both of you. In fact, it helps your whole family. It is not unusual for parents to write a testimonial about how I've saved their marriage or was paramount in the decision to extend their family. One lovely family I helped twice with their babies even said the following:

> *"Hannah and her techniques are amazing. We used her services with our older child at six months old and she turned our lives around then. To be honest, the decision to have a second baby was only firmly sealed when we knew Hannah could advise on newborn babies too!"*
>
> — *PRIYA*

You may, however, have some reasons that won't work. If the reason you are here is only because of one of the following, please question if this is right for you:

- My husband wants me to teach baby to sleep.

- My mother-in-law says my baby is a nightmare and won't look after them.
- My husband wants to do controlled crying to get baby out of our bed; I like co-sleeping: this is a compromise.

These reasons indicate the parent isn't ready for the change, they don't want to change, and they are doing it for someone else. I have learnt through experience that this rarely works. If your heart isn't in the change, you will not apply the three Cs. Your baby will sense you aren't on board with the change and this will make it impossible for them to be.

What are your three reasons for being here?

Insert your reasons into this box:
1
2
3

VISUALISATION: WHERE DO YOU WANT TO GET TO?

Once you have your three reasons for being here, turn these into visions, that is, where you will be at the end of this process.

You might say things like:

- I will have my evenings back as I will be able to pop baby into their cot and walk downstairs and baby will settle themselves to sleep. I will be able to have a meal and a glass of wine with my husband.
- I will have a baby who settles in their cot for naps so I will be able to enjoy some time with my toddler and get some things done.
- My baby won't feed all night so will eat well in the day time. No more making meals that are thrown on the floor!
- My baby will be better at sleeping anywhere so we can book that camping trip.

Post these visions where you see them every day… on the back of your baby's bedroom door… on the fridge. They must remind you, daily, why you are doing this.

There will be times in the process when you feel it isn't working, you want to give up and you find things *so* hard. These visions will keep you motivated, and ensure you cross that finish line and get to the point where these visions become reality.

What are your three visualisations?

Insert your visualisations into this box:
1
2
3

DO YOU HAVE SUPPORT?

In many families, one parent is more involved in the process, more on board, than the other. This is often because one does the lion's share of the nights, while the other does not realise the immense impact of the sleep deprivation. It can also be the other way around and the parent that has been on the sofa for twelve months wants to get back into their bed but the parent that is with baby can't bear to think of sleep training or hearing baby cry. Whatever the reason for one of you being more invested in the process, it can still work. There is one rule, though. The parent that isn't on board must not intervene. You can be less invested; the person implementing the changes can do this on their own; but it won't work if the less invested parent tries to step in, to help, to come and rescue baby or to intervene in the process. The rule is to get on board *or* take a step back.

If partway through the process you see the change in your baby, see the change in your partner, and see that it's working, by all means, offer support but ensure you know the rules and know the process before helping.

It is amazing if both parents are on board. Sharing the process and doing this together as a family always makes it so much easier.

> *"At the time of our training, I had been breastfeeding to sleep for eight months and as such my husband had not had any part to play in getting baby to sleep or back to sleep through the night by co-sleeping. He only agreed to pay the money because I was desperately crying, shattered and we wanted to be sleeping back in the same room!*
>
> *Initially I watched all the videos, read all the material and he had no desire to join me but he understood I needed to do something so I was very much the driver. I would say the key thing here is that although he didn't put the headphones on and watch the videos or instigate the weaning changes, etc., he didn't stand in my way of making the changes myself. It is important to support your partner's wishes even if you don't intrinsically involve yourself in the actions.*
>
> *Move forward four weeks and he asked me to show him what I was doing and how to do it - because he could see it working! He moved back into our room for starters and baby was back in his room! Once he realised that HE could get our son to sleep and HE could go to him in the night and succeed in resettling him that was the game*

changer. It fills you with confidence when you win the battle."

YOUR BABY'S STARTING DIARY

You also need to keep a detailed twenty-four-hour diary *(example in the box below)*. You must include all milk feeds (times or amounts), food (rough amounts), naps (how baby settles and duration), including any false starts. You also need to document overnight wakes (all of them) and what you need to do at each wake.

This starting diary is for use as a reference. There are times when parents think they haven't made any progress. One look at their starting diary, in comparison to their 'now' diary, and they see the huge progress they have made.

Many parents who work with me one-to-one call me and they say, 'This isn't working. I'm not seeing any progress. What am I doing wrong?" According to the diary they sent that morning, baby was awake four times in the night, had two feeds, settled in the cot with a pat, and had four feeds and three meals the day before. Their starting diary from two weeks earlier records eight night-time wakes, six feeds, cuddling to sleep and six feeds in the day. You only need to compare the two to see the progress.

When things improve you soon forget how bad they were. This is your body's brilliant way of protecting you from trauma – a well-known scenario in rehabilitation and I see it time and time again in my programmes too. Referring to previous diary entries is a vital way to keep you motivated and on track. Do not skip this important step.

EXAMPLE DIARY:

Harrison, 8 months

5.47 wake - start the day not interested in milk as feeding in the night
6.15 wanted milk; 2-min feed then happy
7.45 breakfast - yoghurt and fruit (1 teaspoon), bite of toast; refused everything else
8.03 asked for feed; 3 mins; looked dozy
8.45 pram nap on dog walk; cried for 4 mins then 50-min nap
9.14 4-min feed; looked sleepy
10.30 rice cake and peanut butter - nibbled
11.30 lunch - fish pie pouch, had a few sucks and 1/2 a bread stick; water
12.00 4-min feed; fell asleep; wake on transfer to cot; feed again 4 mins; contact nap on me 1 hour
13.15 3-min feed
Play swim
15.00 4-min feed and offered bottle, 2oz taken; short nap on way home in car
17.00 dinner - ate well; mash and veg puree and fruit after
18.00 bath, 3-min feed after
PJ play
Books
Feed to sleep (12 mins, sleepy)
7.04 wake on transfer; feed again, didn't want, slept on me
8.30 managed to transfer
9.15 wake; rock back to sleep
10.15 wake and feed (co-sleep from here)
Feed at: 1; 2.15; 4; 4.30; 5
5.55 wake for the day; not interested in milk

Summary:

Milk feeds: 17
Overnight wakes: 8
Naps: 3 and 2 dozy episodes.

Pop your diary in this box so you can refer back to it – to see how far you have come.

YOUR BABY'S SAFE SLEEP PLACE

To move forward you need to pinpoint your baby's safe sleep place to *go* to sleep. This is the sleep technique you currently resort to, to get baby to sleep. This will differ from baby to baby but some common ones are:

- Feeding to sleep
- Rocking to sleep
- Bouncing on a gym ball or the edge of the bed
- Rocking in a rocking chair
- Being rocked in a pram or crib
- Being walked around over your shoulder
- Co-sleeping and cuddling
- Contact napping on a sofa or in bed

Your baby's safe sleep place may change from person to person. You might feed to sleep but your partner might bounce. It also might differ between naps and bed time, with naps happening in the pram but bed time happening with feeding. It is ok to have more than one safe sleep place. The point is that you have identified how you currently get baby to sleep, which you will move forward from with this programme. Soon you and your baby will have a new safe sleep place.

What is your baby's 'safe sleep place'? Write it in this box:

SETTING UP THE SLEEP ROOM

For a sleep training programme, you need a sleep room. This sleep room raises a lot of questions and issues for many parents.

In this room must be your baby's cot and a mattress or futon for you to sleep on. Your baby will initially sleep on this too so it can't be an air bed, for safety reasons, and needs to be big enough for the two of you. If it's easier to start the sleep training in your room, using your bed as the 'mattress' and your baby's cot or travel cot in there too, that's fine but **you must have both a cot and a bed or mattress in the same room**. This is vital for the process.

Some people use a travel cot mattress or even a duvet on the floor, due to limited space. The disadvantage of this is it isn't as comfortable for you. There may well be points in the process when you choose to co-sleep or stay in the room with your baby while you address the overnights so you must have a way of staying comfortably in the sleep room with your baby.

SLEEP QUESTIONNAIRE:

Answer the following questions with a score. You will repeat this a couple of times during the process, which allows you to see how much progress you are making and which areas still need work. Be honest, pop the answer in the space at the end, and then forget about it. We will revisit it later.

Score each statement in the following way...

- **Not an issue at all = 1 point**
- **Occasionally an issue = 2 points**
- **More of an issue than not = 3 points**
- **This is my baby = 4 points**

1. My baby relies on me to help them go to sleep at every nap and bedtime. [___]
2. My baby will only contact nap. [___]
3. My baby wakes every time I try to transfer them. [___]
4. Bed times are a struggle and I end up in their room for over an hour. [___]
5. My baby's day is unpredictable. I never know what to expect.[___]

6. I feel anxious that my baby doesn't get enough sleep. [___]
7. My baby is fussy with their food and is not weaning onto solids. (Score one point if baby isn't weaning yet) [___]
8. I am up multiple times in the night helping my baby get back to sleep. [___]
9. No one else can help me settle my baby. It's all down to me. [___]
10. I don't feel like I can cope with my baby's sleep any more. [___]
11. We have false starts or short naps every day. [___]

Put your answer here (total score): [___]

CHECKLIST: are you ready for module two?

Before moving to the next module *(Daytime Changes)* have you:

- Noted your baby's safe place to sleep?
- Prepared your baby's sleep space with a bed (or mattress) **and** a cot in the same room?
- Written your three reasons for being here and your visualisations of where you will get to?
- Completed the questionnaire and noted the score?
- Completed a twenty-four-hour diary and summarised the feeds/sleep?

Do not move to module two until the above is completed.

MODULE TWO: DAYTIME CHANGES

PLEASE READ THE WHOLE CHAPTER BEFORE MAKING ANY CHANGES.

WHY MAKE DAYTIME CHANGES FIRST?

When parents contact me, it is undoubtedly the night times that cause them the most stress: no one wants to be up many times a night to settle a baby. If they have tried any kind of sleep training before, they have usually (and understandably) focused on the night-time settles as this is where they want the changes to happen. This has often resulted in lots of crying and the programme not working.

With CALM you will start with the daytime changes, even if these aren't where you feel your biggest issues lie. Parents who contact me often feel that their naptime or bedtime routines are working perfectly. Perhaps their baby settles well on a bottle, or naps are at the same time in the pram each day. They feel day times are not troublesome for them, and the only issues lie in the night times.

If your baby does not go into their cot fully awake and settle without any help at nap and bedtimes, they will not be able to achieve this when they wake overnight. Even subtle routine issues in the day time can have an effect on the overnights, such as milk feeds close to nap times, or baby always sleeping in a different place from a night-time sleep. Therefore, it is vital we start with the day times and ensure they work well - before tackling the nights.

On top of this, I think everyone would agree that it is much easier to practise new things in the day time when you are able to function well. Few people decide to set an alarm and take on a new challenge at three am. Your patience and ability to learn would be compromised. If you practise the new sleep technique in the day time you can perfect it before moving to night times. Once you are confident with your new settling technique in the day time, you can easily progress to use this overnight and will be much more likely to remember the three Cs (calm, consistent, confident) when doing it.

Also, it is much easier to judge a baby's tiredness and readiness to sleep when they haven't already been asleep. The next few chapters will give you tips and checks to decide if your baby is tired enough. They will advise you how to get baby ready for bed and nap time, including active play, entertaining, burning off energy, and looking for tiredness signs – all things that are easy to do when baby is awake. It is much harder to spot tiredness signs in the middle of the night when baby has already been asleep.

Finally, it is one skill to go from being awake (and tired) to asleep, but a completely different skill to go from being asleep, to awake and back to sleep again. This will come but it is harder for your baby to master. They need to master the former first.

It is also true that the night times often get better with just the daytime changes[1]. Sleep training a baby takes a lot of energy, and I don't want to put pressure on you to make changes all through the full twenty-four-hour period. For most this won't be manageable

---

Note 1: *This natural improvement is typically seen in about 75% of my sleep programmes. Some parents don't see improvement in the night-time changes until they start to tackle them. If you find this is the case for you then progress to the night-time changes more quickly – these are all found in module three – but not before you complete the daytime changes.*

DAYTIME CHANGES: PART ONE,

AIMING FOR A MORE PREDICTABLE DAY - YOUR BABY'S (*SHUSH*) *R-O-U-T-I-N-E*

Parents often shy away from the thought of putting in any kind of routine. They either feel they'll be stuck in the house clock watching, or worry the routine will be the reason they will be stuck in the house, or breastfeeding will fail, or their baby will not put on weight well or will drop through their centiles as they absolutely must 'feed on demand'. For these reasons, I don't like using the word 'routine' with parents.

Let me say right now that none of these extremes are true. But, in any case, rather than 'routine' let's just call this a 'more predictable day'.

We need to do this first. A more predictable day gives you a way to tell if your baby is hungry or tired. Predictability gives you time to practise getting your baby to go to sleep without feeding, confident they aren't hungry. Predictability also gives you freedom. Once you know when baby will feed and sleep, you can plan around those times and do lovely things with your baby.

The table below gives you your baby's routine by age. Remember to refer back to this each month or so as your baby's routine will naturally change as they get older.

In your Sleep Well Hub there are full, downloadable routines. Please follow the QR code at the front of the book to access these.

ROUTINES FOR EACH AGE

3-6 months	**6-8 months when on 3 meals***	**7-10 months**	**10-12 months**	**12-18 months**	**plus**
6-7am Wake & milk	6-7am Wake & milk	6-7am Wake & milk	6-7am Wake & milk	6-7am Wake & milk (if they still want milk)	6-7am Wake
Milk feeds every 3-4 hrs Follow the EASA routine (Eat, Activity, Sleep, Activity) Around 7.30pm Penultimate feed Biggest awake time 9.30pm bedtime feed Awake time Bed when tired between 9 and 10	Breakfast 1 hour later	Breakfast 1 hour later	Breakfast 1 hour later	Breakfast 1 hour later	Breakfast
	Morning nap	Morning nap	If still awake 1 hour later a little more breakfast	Snack mid-morning; short morning nap if they still need it	Snack
	Wake, play & milk mid-morning	Wake & milk or snack (change to a snack by 8 months)	Approximate 30 mins morning nap		
	Lunch 1 hr later (11.30/12)	Lunch 1 hr later (11.30/12)	Lunch (12ish)	Lunch	Lunch
	Lunch nap	Lunch nap	Lunch nap	Lunch nap	Lunch nap until no longer needed
	Wake & milk feed mid afternoon	Wake & milk feed mid afternoon	Wake & milk or snack mid afternoon	Snack	Evening meal
	Evening meal about 4.30/5	Evening meal 1 hr later (4.30)	Evening meal	Evening meal	Milk from a beaker or snack before bath
	Shorter nap either before or after evening meal				Bed
	Bedtime routine: milk minimum 2 hours after evening meal and 20 min before bed time	Bedtime routine: milk 30 min before bed time	Bedtime routine: milk 30 min before bed time	Bedtime routine: milk can be before bath, and can switch to cereal or yoghurt approaching 18 months	

*Find *routines for weaning babies transitioning from 1 to 2 to 3 meals in the weaning section and also your Sleep Well Hub.*

Your daytime routine includes baby's daytime milk feeds, meals, and snacks, as well as naps in between these. There are no specific times for naps. This must go on their cues because you cannot predict when your baby will be tired (more to come on this). Feeds and meals do have times, however, as this gives your baby opportunities for calories at regular intervals.

Some babies fall into this new routine easily, while some take a few days; it shouldn't take more than a week to succeed in having more predictability with these daytime changes.

Your baby's sleep needs will reduce as they get older and nap times will change. A newborn might sleep up to nineteen hours a day, whereas a twelve-month-old only needs about twelve hours sleep out of twenty-four. This gives them time to learn, grow and develop. It is often a tricky time for parents; one minute you think you've 'cracked it' and have a perfect routine and then it no longer works for you and your baby.

WHAT NAPS MIGHT YOUR BABY NEED?

Every baby is different but below is a rough guide of what to expect.

3-6 months	3-5 naps	Morning: 45 mins - 1 hour Lunch: 1-2 hours (maybe across 2 shorter 45-minute naps) Afternoon: 45 mins Possible power nap later in the evening Some babies don't manage to stretch their naps until they are weaned onto solids.
6-9 months	2-3 naps	Morning: 45 min - 1.5 hours Afternoon: 1-2 hours Possible third nap: 20 mins max (most drop this by 8 months and move to 2 longer naps)
8-10 months	2 naps	Most babies manage 2 equal sleeps of 1-1.5 hours mid-morning and mid-afternoon
10-14 months	2 naps	Morning: 30 mins (as this moves later, you'll need to shorten it further) Afternoon: 1-2 hours
11 months – 2 years	1 nap	Lunch: 1-3 hours. Babies' sleep needs see a big reduction at 18 months. At this point they usually need to reduce their day sleep.
2-3 years	0-1 naps. When your toddler drops their nap varies from toddler to toddler. Shorten it when bed time gets harder, or later.	When they drop their daytime sleep most toddlers increase their overnight sleep to 11-12 hours. Until that point, they need less than this. When they eventually drop their nap, they might still need a short one some days. Ensure this is only short so as not to affect night-time sleep.

HOW TO KNOW WHEN TO DROP NAPS AS YOUR BABY GETS OLDER

Each transition (three to two naps; two to one nap; dropping all daytime naps) is tricky. It is never a smooth ride. Notice your baby's sleep cues. If they do not show signs of being tired, don't put them to bed. If they start to protest when you put them to bed, wait longer before attempting to put them down, especially if they're happy to play for longer.

TRANSITIONS *BEFORE* THE 'TWO TO ONE' NAP TRANSITION

For all transitions prior to the 'two to one' nap transition, your baby's naps get later. This happens naturally as they become able to extend their awake windows. Start putting them to bed later for every nap. Encouraging bigger awake windows can make settling easier and encourage the routine change. This will naturally make the final nap later, which you will then need to shorten. The final nap will get progressively later and shorter, until baby only needs a thirty-second shut-eye to get through to bed time. Try and avoid bringing bed time earlier.

THE 'TWO TO ONE' AND 'ONE TO ZERO' NAP TRANSITIONS

When they transition from two sleeps to one, you will have to cut down their morning sleep if they are no longer tired for their lunch sleep. With this transition, the important thing is that baby is tired after lunch so you can get an afternoon sleep in without it having an impact on bed time. You will find, as they get older, they need more awake time before bed time (which should always be the longest awake time of the day in any baby). Rather than cutting down the lunch nap, which will remain, cut down the morning nap until they're ready to drop it altogether.

The transition between one nap and no nap is often tricky. For a long time, your toddler might need a nap some days but not on others. You could move to 'quiet time' at this point. Put a film on and it is fine if they just watch quietly. If they sometimes need a sleep, let them. I strongly advise keeping naps short in order not to affect bed time.

It is rarely a clean transition when your baby is dropping naps. It is very normal for your toddler to need an occasional short nap for many months after they have 'dropped' their nap.

SOME CONSIDERATIONS WHEN AIMING FOR A MORE PREDICTABLE DAY

Parents are often surprised at how few milk feeds I advise. **I may well be advising many fewer milk feeds than you are currently doing.** Many parents are concerned the baby won't have enough milk or calories if they reduce the number of milk feeds. Please rest easy, whether your baby is bottle-fed or breastfed. As soon as you reduce the number of feeds in twenty-four hours, the volume of each individual feed increases. Breastfed babies become more interested in the feeds, less distracted and spend more time on the breast. Bottle-fed babies start to drink more at each feed.

Another consideration is **aiming for overnight hours that are far too long.** You've been playing, feeding, rocking, bouncing, and changing poonamis for twelve hours, you are ready to get baby to bed. Unfortunately, this will result in early mornings, split nights or poor overnight sleep. A baby's night-time hours are around ten hours when they are still napping. Babies rarely need twelve hours sleep overnight and this is even more true of 'poor sleepers'. If you are reading this book it is doubtful you have a 'good, high sleep needs baby' on your hands.

There is another good reason for a longer day time of fourteen hours. Once fully weaned your baby needs three meals, and one to four milk feeds (depending on their age). Some might need snacks, and their naps too. This is possible in twelve hours, but everything would be very close together. When meals and milk feeds are close together, your baby does not have enough time to get hungry and they won't feed well at meals or milk feeds, which is exactly what they need to sleep well at night. Before starting CALM your baby might be in bed for twelve or even thirteen hours, especially if they're up a lot in the night. To establish a good day time, you need to ensure no more than ten hours in bed overnight, including any night-time wakes.[2]

Note 2: This is taken from bed time, irrespective of overnight wakes or feeds so an 8 pm bed time means a 6 am wake up.

As for **total duration of sleep**, it is tempting to calculate every minute your baby sleeps. Most parents have apps for this and can tell me every second baby has slept for the past six months. These calculations are often thrown around NCT and parenting groups almost as a set of top trump card statistics. How long your baby sleeps initially is irrelevant. The only thing that matters is how baby settles, not how long they sleep for or even where they sleep. Some babies sleep less for a time, while they adapt. This will regulate further into the course.

Because of these sleep calculations parents often try to get their babies to sleep too soon. For the sleep technique to work, your baby needs to be tired. The technique in itself won't make your baby more tired, and nor will the sleep triggers. One of the main reasons for a baby to protest against sleep is that they are not tired. Often, parents put this down to baby being over-tired, but it is much more common for baby to be under-tired (not tired enough). Baby being tired and ready to sleep is one of the most important parts of this process. It is often the 'magic key' that parents discover.

> *"Day two of the free sleep workshop and my baby is settling with the new technique within a few minutes each time. I feel the biggest thing that has helped is ensuring baby is tired, I've increased the awake windows, ensuring lots of active play and this means baby is actually tired. Your window and mirror trick is genius!"*

(You can read about the window and mirror trick later.)

Be careful not to **get sleep cues and hunger cues confused**. They can often be similar, especially in smaller babies or babies who have previously been fed to sleep. Babies can often face rub, root, look for comfort, cry, and be hard to entertain when they are hungry *or* tired, making it hard to ascertain when baby is ready to sleep. It isn't at all unusual for a parent to misread these signs and feed baby, and baby immediately falls asleep, indicating they were tired rather than hungry.

So… how can you tell if your baby is tired and ready to sleep, rather than hungry? This is all down to the predictable day. Having a good routine means separating feeding and sleep. Once you have managed this, if your baby shows any of the above signals when they have had their meal, snack or recent milk feed, you can be confident to get them to sleep without feeding. We will talk more about spotting sleep signals later in this module.

Don't worry about how many naps your baby has. The routine includes the 'average' but, as I have already stressed, no baby is an average baby. Some babies might have four short naps rather than two longer ones. The number of naps might vary from day to day. Again, that will consolidate and become more predictable once your baby can bridge the sleep cycles. For now, go on their sleep cues (more to come on this) and how they get to sleep. The rest will follow.

Finally, **let's talk about power naps**. A very short nap (sometimes as short as ten seconds) can help when babies are transitioning through naps. When Henry, my youngest, was twelve months old, I used to give him a ten-second nap on the way to the childminder for the morning. If I did this, he could last until the time I collected him at midday. If I missed this ten-second nap, he would fall asleep in his lunch at 11.30 and that would be 'game over' for his lovely long lunchtime nap when he came home. You can also use this if your baby can't quite make it until bed time; taking them into a dark room and cuddling to sleep, or taking a little pram walk to give them a quick shut-eye, even for a few seconds, can help see them through the final two hours before bed.

While there is benefit to these short naps, there is also equal risk. It probably comes as no surprise that these short naps are often called danger naps. As with Henry, even ten seconds can prevent a baby being able to fall asleep again. Eyes closing on a bedtime feed, baby nodding off in the car, or even relaxing on your shoulder on the way up to the bedroom, can mean your baby struggles to go back off to sleep. Parents can describe this as being 'over-tired' but it is cause they have had a short power nap (or danger) and can't then get back to sleep.

Consider power naps in adults. I'm sure you've been there – sitting on the sofa watching TV and your eyes are still open but you can feel that you're falling asleep. You think, 'This is silly; I need to go to bed.' But when you get up to bed you can't go back to sleep again for ages. It's frustrating, isn't it? That is how your baby feels when they have a power nap leading up to bed or nap time. When this happens, they tell you very clearly that they're not tired by screaming if you try to get them to sleep.

Key Points:

- Do not worry about a reduction in milk feeds: your baby will naturally take more at each feed.
- You must stick to a maximum of ten hours of overnight sleep.
- Don't worry about total duration of sleep: it is only important how baby *gets* to sleep, not where they sleep or for how long they sleep.
- Don't confuse sleeping and hunger cues.
- It doesn't matter how many naps your baby has. It might change from day to day and depends on how tired they are.
- Watch out for (or utilise) power naps.

BEFORE BED AND NAPTIME ROUTINE

As a part of your new predictable day, look at the time leading up to bed and nap times, starting with your baby's night-time bedtime routine.

BED TIME: YOUR BABY'S NIGHT-TIME ROUTINE

There is a lot of misinformation out there about bedtime routines. It isn't unusual for parents to describe their routine in infinite detail, often starting two hours before bed time with after-dinner play, bath time, lights being dimmed, a massage, stories, ambient music, the same story, daddy saying goodnight, milk with dimmed lights, then a little rock while they sing the same tune... the list goes on.

I am a firm believer in consistency. I also agree that babies love to know what's happening. However, if a baby relies on two hours of wind down time and a perfectly formed, never deviated from routine just to go to sleep, they will never learn to be a good and independent sleeper.

At the end of the programme, you want your baby to be able to go to sleep when tired, no matter the situation, no matter what's been going on up to that point and with only a couple of minutes of sleep triggers to indicate sleep is expected of them. We also want them to be able to carry this skill to other places other than their cot.

As well as that, I don't want you to need to shut yourself away and complete a ritual every single evening just to get your little one to sleep. No matter how much parents love their babies, I don't know any parent who wouldn't find this frustrating and mundane.

If this is you, we are going to switch up your bedtime routine to include play, fun, variation, and family time. Throw away the ties to your current routine. This can be a fun time for your family, a time to visit friends, have family over, be in the garden in the summer, go out to the pub for dinner in the evening, and your baby still… yes, still… will be able to sleep at the end of it.

To manage this, the first thing is to know that it is not important that the lead-up to bed time remains the same. Some nights you might give a bath; some nights not. Some nights you might be out for the evening and take your baby's pyjamas and bottle out with you. Some nights you might have family over, nip baby up before they arrive for a wash and change, and then bring them back downstairs to join you for the first part of the evening.

There are only two things that must be the same each night: firstly, your baby's bedtime milk must be away from the sleep room, with a minimum of thirty minutes **active** play after they have finished it. Secondly, the sleep triggers (your mini bedtime routine) must remain the same for both nap-time settling and bedtime settling.

What a night-time routine might look like:

- Eat their evening meal.
- Go upstairs.
- Bath/change/wash.
- Back downstairs, massage and pyjamas.
- Closer to bed time, milk feed away from their sleep room. **Do not** let them fall asleep at all. This might be in a few smaller feeds.
- Once fed, have some awake play time (active, running about, nappy off time, **not** relaxing) until they are tired.
- When they show signs of being tired, make your baby look out of the window or into a mirror. If they are still grumpy, this usually means they are tired enough for sleep!
- When your baby is ready for sleep go to the sleep room.
- Do the mini bedtime routine sleep triggers.
- Get your baby to sleep using the sleep technique.

Or your bedtime might look like this:

- Go out for dinner.
- Put pyjamas on at friend's house.
- Play time with family and friends.
- Baby has bedtime milk in a busy environment. It is very stop-start but they finish the milk.
- You head home, keeping baby awake.
- Once home, burn off the last bit of energy with playtime.
- When they show signs of being tired, usually characterised by grumpiness, make your baby look out of the window or into a mirror. If they are still grumpy, this usually means they are tired enough for sleep!
- When your baby is ready for sleep go to the sleep room.
- Do the mini bedtime routine sleep triggers.
- Get your baby to sleep using the sleep technique.

In both examples, baby has the same mini bedtime routine for the last few minutes before bed and milk at least thirty minutes before bed time.

YOUR BABY'S SLEEP TRIGGERS (MINI BEDTIME ROUTINE)

I keep talking about your mini bedtime routine, so what is it? This is simply a few sleep triggers you use to get your baby to sleep. Use the same ones whenever you settle your baby in the sleep training room to indicate to your baby that sleep is expected of them. You will use them in the same order for nap time and bed time. They will remain the same throughout the whole sleep training process.

Sleep triggers may vary slightly from baby to baby, but some common ones are listed below. Pick a **minimum of four and a maximum of six**. Use the same ones, in the same order, **every time** you do the sleep technique in the sleep room.

- Putting on your baby's sleeping bag or swaddle
- Closing the curtains or blinds
- Singing a song
- Saying goodnight to the birdies/teddies/a picture of family
- Putting on music or white noise
- Saying a sleep cue ("sleepy time", "good night baby", "time for sleep")
- Giving your baby a comforter or dummy if they have one. Don't introduce this as a new trigger. *Only use a comforter if your baby is old enough to have one safely.*

Do these things in the same way, in the same order, whether it's nap time or bed time. Whoever puts your baby to sleep in the sleep room needs to do the same. These triggers will indicate to your baby that it is sleep time and they will soon recognise these triggers. You will use them for overnight settles too, once you get to that part.

FORGET ABOUT AWAKE WINDOWS: HOW TO DECIDE WHEN YOUR BABY IS READY TO SLEEP

There is far too much contradictory information about sleep. Parents have read how not getting enough sleep can affect development or that their baby will be damaged if they don't get enough sleep. In twenty years of working with families and babies, most of whom are 'poor' sleepers, most of whom get less than 'average' sleep, I have never once met a baby with any kind of developmental delay or issue because of their lack of sleep.

Because of this anxiety, nearly every family that approaches me for sleep help is trying to get their baby to sleep more than they need. I hear of parents trying for hours to rock, sing, and coax baby to go to sleep, all in vain. This results in the baby protesting against naps, struggling with early mornings, and having false starts in the evening. It makes the settling to sleep much, much harder.

It is far more common for parents to try to get baby to sleep too soon, than for baby to be over-tired.

Read and internalise this statement. It is so very important to the process.

SO... HOW TO DECIDE WHEN TO PUT YOUR BABY TO SLEEP

Wake windows, by-the-clock routines, average awake times… forget them. The worst question for me on parenting forums is, 'I need awake windows for my ten-month-old, please.' That question is as difficult to answer as, 'Can you please let me know when I'll next be hungry?' It is impossible for someone else to judge. You must go on *your* baby, the same way as you'd listen to *your* digestive system to know when to eat. Awake windows can vary from day to day, depending on so many factors: how well your baby slept overnight, how active they are, how long their nap was, and if they are growing or learning. There is no way you can go by the clock for baby's sleep. Therefore, it's important to learn your baby's sleep cues to know when they need to go to sleep.

To ensure this is possible, have lots of active play leading up to bed time and nap time. No relaxing. We have already eliminated the bedtime routines that instruct you to turn lights down, have relaxing music playing, relaxing stories and no excitement. Do the opposite. I want you to treat the time leading up to bed time and nap time as fun, active play. Play with favourite toys. Have a fun bath with lots of splashing, then run around after your baby.

There are several reasons for this. Firstly, research sho' the endorphins released during a fun activity aid sleep. Secondly, it is much easier to judge when your baby is tired when they are active and having fun. Finally, they are less likely to sneak in a little power nap which can be damaging leading up to bed and nap times.

When your little one stops being interested in playing, doesn't want their favourite activity or toys, and isn't happy being entertained – when they no longer see being up as 'fun' – this is when they are ready for bed. Burn off that last bit of energy, get the endorphins circulating. Make sure there is no room for a little power nap. Ensure baby is tired before you start the technique. At this point you can use the 'window and mirror trick' as a final check (see below). This way, you will prevent a lot of unnecessary battles.

The window and mirror trick

This is a 'final check' of whether your baby is tired enough for sleep. They've had their bedtime feed, have been playing with their toys, and have needed lots of entertainment. Baby is increasingly grumpy, less interested in playing and isn't interested in their favourite toys. Take them towards the sleep room and get them to look out of the window or into a mirror. If your baby is interested and wants to play with 'that baby in the mirror' then they aren't tired enough for sleep. If, however, your baby isn't interested in that baby in the mirror, turns away, or is still grumpy, it's time for sleep.

UNDER-TIRED VERSUS OVER-TIRED

When a baby makes a big protest against going to sleep, it is far more common for it to be because baby isn't tired enough (under-tired). It is rare for a baby to be genuinely 'over-tired' unless there has been a power nap. The most common scenario is for baby to get sleepy on the bedtime feed. If they are very tired when they have the bedtime feed and momentarily close their eyes or even have a long stare, this 'power nap' can prevent them from being able to go back to sleep – for up to an hour in a small baby and much longer in an older baby. This is why it is vital to have a minimum of thirty minutes of active play time after the bedtime feed. If baby gets a second wind, it is important you burn off that energy before attempting bed time. Personally, I'd much rather have a happy, playing baby up for another hour than a baby screaming for an hour because they aren't tired enough to go to sleep.

Never try to get a baby who is playing happily to sleep. If your baby is happy, they are not ready to sleep.

If this means a much later bed time or bigger awake windows in the early days, go with this. You can address this down the line by shortening naps. If your baby's bed time is too late for you, shorten the final nap. Remember, you need to be up ten hours after bed time so don't make it too early.

DAYTIME CHANGES: PART TWO

FEEDING AND SLEEP

THE LINK BETWEEN FOOD AND SLEEP

I noticed the link between feeding and sleep long before I started helping babies to sleep well professionally. From 2000-2008 I divided my time between running drop-in feeding clinics for government Sure Start children's centres, taking clinical sessions for the National Nutritional Clinic in Richmond as their Principle Paediatric Nutritional Therapist, plus my role as a nanny. My I offered a unique combination of medical and nutritional knowledge and my clinics were always busy.

When I was helping parents with weaning and nutrition I noticed the definite link between feeding and sleep. Parents came to me because baby was not putting on weight, wasn't feeding well in the day time, was fussy with food or was having issues with weaning. The one thing they all had in common was poor sleep.

I unintentionally started my sleep training journey with these families. There was no way I could resolve their babies' feeding issues if I didn't address sleep. Once I addressed both issues, the babies slept and ate well. Because of my success in addressing these families' feeding and sleep issues, people started to contact me about sleep; at the time there was no such thing as a sleep trainer or sleep specialist so my services were sought after. Just as I had been passed around the golfers as a sought-after nanny, I was now passed around the Richmond NCT groups as a sought-after sleep specialist for babies. I was 'more than just a sleep trainer' and helped hundreds of families one-to-one for the next fifteen years. I rarely advertised. My business grew organically, mainly by word of mouth and I reached the ceiling of how many parents I could help.

Nowadays, parents predominantly come to me for sleep, but to address sleep I must look at feeding. I think this is why other sleep programmes often fail: feeding, weaning and nutrition are often overlooked or misunderstood.

If a baby doesn't feed well in the day time, you won't get them to nap well. Feeding through the night must also be addressed before they will sleep through. No amount of sleep training will address that.

Also, certain foods can affect sleep both positively and negatively. Some foods aid sleep. They have nutrients that encourage sleep and are gentle on the tummy. Other foods might cause wind, tummy ache and issues like constipation, which all have a negative effect on sleep. Your baby's diet needs to contribute positively to their sleep.

STAGE ONE WEANING

A introduction to weaning for babies who are not yet on three meals

Initially, solid food is an **extra to their milk feeds.** Most of their calories and nutrients should still come from their milk feeds, which slowly changes over the first three to six months of weaning.

The best time of day to start weaning is around an hour after their morning milk feed, when they are not overly hungry and shouldn't be tired. It also extends the gap between their first two milk feeds (once they are swallowing a little) which allows more time for their morning nap.

Here are your baby's routines when introducing one, two and three meals.

(These are downloadable in your Sleep Well Hub via the QR code.)

One meal:	**Two meals:**	**Three meals:**
Wake and milk feed (assuming 6 am)	Wake and milk feed (6 am)	Wake and milk feed
One hour later, breakfast	Breakfast	Breakfast
Sleep	Sleep	Sleep
10 am milk feed	10 am milk feed	Mid-morning (time is not as important now) milk feed
Sleep		
	11.30 lunch	Lunch
1 pm milk feed		
Sleep	Sleep	Sleep
4 pm milk feed	2 pm milk feed	Mid-afternoon milk feed
Short sleep 5.30 penultimate feed	5.30 milk feed (penultimate)	Very short nap
7.30 bedtime feed 8 pm bed	7.30 bedtime feed 8 pm bed	Evening meal (instead of penultimate feed)
One feed overnight		Bedtime feed and bed

I advise working up to the three meal routine by six-and-a-half to seven months. It doesn't matter how much food your baby eats, just that you offer it at those times.

FIRST FOODS

I always advise starting with high-calorie, high-nutrient foods. I also advise starting with savoury foods so as not to encourage a sweet tooth. Vegetables can be mixed with a little avocado, coconut or baby cereal so baby has the benefit of higher-calorie foods.

Vegetable foods: Carrot, avocado, sweet potato, parsnip

Carbohydrate foods: Sweet potato, lentils, cereal

Protein foods: Chicken, lentils (lentils are a good source of both carbohydrate and protein)

Fruits: Pear and prune (if at all constipated)

Fats: Avocado, coconut cream, olive oil and later progress to nut butter

If you decide to start weaning before six months, you must stick to vegetable, carbohydrate and fat-based foods. Protein must not be introduced until close to six months.

FIRST MEALS

Breakfast: Start with avocado or sweet potato and coconut or baby cereal mixed with a vegetable puree (from the list above) made with formula or expressed breast milk.

Lunch: A mix of fifty percent avocado and fifty percent banana, papaya or pear. Use papaya or pear if your baby has ever been constipated. I would be happy for every baby to have avocado every day for the first three months of weaning.

Evening meal: A mix of protein, carbohydrates and vegetables from the list above. In the recipes in the Sleep

Well Hub, the lentil bake is great for the first evening meal. Just omit the spices the first time you make it.

Other important points to remember when starting weaning:

- **Introduce savoury foods first** so as not to encourage a sweet tooth. I have never known a child not to like sweet flavours but plenty who refuse to eat vegetables; introduce the foods this way round for the best possible chance of your child liking all foods.
- Research shows that your baby needs to **try a different flavour up to seventeen times before liking it.** It is not unusual for them to turn their nose up at each new flavour. Initially (for the first week or so) they will eat very little, sometimes just a taste; this is normal.
- In the first three weeks keep offering the same amount of milk (if your baby is roughly on a three- to four-hourly feeding routine already). They may take less at the feeds at which you offer the solids but the majority of their calories should still be from milk. Your baby will naturally reduce their milk feeds as they take more solid food.

STAGE TWO WEANING

MOVING FORWARD – INTRODUCING FAVOURITE FAMILY RECIPES

Once your baby is eating three proper meals a day consisting of the four important food groups (protein, carbohydrate, vegetables and fruits, and fats) their milk feeds will naturally decrease. Their milk requirement drops to around 18oz (600ml) of formula, or approximately three breastfeeds in any twenty-four hours. I advise running on the three meal routine by seven months.

In stage two weaning you can introduce more exciting flavours and textures into your baby's diet. You can start to introduce small lumps into the puree, herbs and spices into the recipes, and finger foods.

FAVOURITE FAMILY RECIPES

You can access all my favourite family recipes in your Sleep Well Hub via the QR code. My recipes are (roughly) a third protein, a third carbohydrate and a third vegetables. Then there are always fats added.

These recipes are tasty enough for the whole family to eat. If you eat them you can add some salt to your portion. It is also important to get your baby used to your own recipes.

MOVING ON WITH FEEDING AND WEANING – FOR ALL BABIES

In the age-based routines you will see meal times and milk feed times. It is important you stick to these times and avoid extra snacks, milk feeds or altering times for meals. It is also vital to move away from 'feeding on demand'. All the routines offer plenty of opportunity for your baby to have calories, if hungry. It is common for babies to be offered twice as many feeds or snacks during the day in the hope that they will not need milk overnight, for example. This is rarely the case. The more often a baby is offered extra milk or food, the less likely they are to eat at the times you want them to.

Once you have your (rough) meal and feed times, you then have an order of the day. This will make your day more predictable. It is normal to feel nervous about these changes, especially if you have been feeding on demand up until now. Moving forward from this can feel daunting. Parents often think, or have been told, that feeding less will mean baby will take fewer calories. This is untrue. Babies take what they need. Whether they feed little and often, or take more but at less frequent intervals, they will take the same amount. The difference is that the latter gives you time to fit naps and awake time between feeds. It also means baby can sleep for longer periods in the night, because the bigger the feed gaps in the day, the bigger the feed gaps overnight.

FEEDING ON DEMAND

Most families are 'feeding on demand' when they contact me. This is perhaps in relation to solid food – offering snacks 'on demand' through the day – or, more commonly, with milk. Parents offer bottles, or the breast, or a combination throughout the day and often the night too.

To achieve your aim of baby sleeping well, you must move away from all aspects of feeding on demand. This is especially important with milk. Do not ignore this. One of the biggest reasons for the programme not working or for a parent finding it hard to move forward is baby being allowed to feed 'when they really want it' or 'when they ask'.

For a baby or toddler to learn that they can't feed overnight, or at bed time, or close to nap time (often the times they most want the breast or bottle for comfort) they must learn that they don't get fed on demand. Babies love consistency. If you aren't consistent with the change, it is impossible for your baby to learn what is expected of them. If, however, your baby only has milk when you offer it, never when they 'demand', they soon get used to this new way of feeding. This removes all confusion for both baby and you.

It can be hard to move forward from feeding on demand (whether that is breast or bottle), just like it was for Robyn in the testimonial below. Many parents think their baby won't adapt, they won't be able to master the changes, and their baby will take less milk and drop feeds. This isn't the case.

Babies adapt well, just as Robyn states. Give the changes a few days and you will see that your baby takes the same amount of milk.

“*After learning the changes I would need to make with the programme, as an anxious first-time parent, I was initially apprehensive about the new routine Hannah had recommended for us. I thought my child couldn't possibly adapt to a feeding routine after having fed on demand until this point. He rarely finished his bottles, sometimes only managing 1-2oz, and cried and resisted every nap or sleep time. Once we started I found myself texting Hannah throughout the day, anxious that he wouldn't take enough milk with the bigger gaps between feeds, and pessimistic, thinking that this plan wouldn't work. My 'I know best' attitude wasn't really helping with the process.*

Hannah reassured me that if I was consistent and committed to the plan then I would see results in a few days. Sure enough, after sticking to it, in a few days we had our son feeding less regularly and drinking more because of it. We even had to top his bottles up. He was also seemingly enjoying the new sleep techniques we were using. I had my doubts for sure, but seeing some results so early on made me feel instantly reassured; it's amazing how easily babies can adapt! Seeing such early signs of improvement makes me look forward to the next few weeks of Hannah's course, and excited as to the possibilities of what we will achieve for both us and our son. I can hand on heart say since starting the course I feel so much more relaxed. I've gone from hating putting my son down for a nap to enjoying it and feeling quite confident about it too.

— ROBYN WARD

REDUCTION IN QUANTITY OF MILK FEEDS

The table is very typical of the comparison between Day One and Day Ten. It is easy to measure in bottle-fed babies but the same happens with breastfed babies – baby just becomes more interested in the feeds you leave in. Not only does the new routine save on sterilising (and often waste) if bottle-feeding, it also allows time for naps between the feeds and sleeping more continuously at night. Baby also has time to get hungry so weaning is easier, as you can fit meals between the milk feeds.

Milk feeds pre-starting:	Milk feeds ten days later:
6 am 2oz 8 am 1oz 9.30 2.5oz 12 pm 2oz 1.45 1oz 3 pm 2oz 5 pm 3oz 7 pm 3.5oz 9.30 2oz 00.30 5oz 01.45 4oz 5 am 3oz	6 am 5oz 9.30 4oz 12.30 5oz 4 pm 6oz 19.15 6oz 1 am 6oz
= 30oz in 12 feeds	= 31oz in 5 feeds

TIPS FOR STOPPING FEEDING ON DEMAND

When a baby feeds on demand, it is often because they are tired, bored, need comfort, entertainment or attention, need a rest, or of course for calories. To move to a 'feed when offered' routine at the times in your routines for each age, you need to move away from this. Your baby will find it impossible to learn why they can sometimes feed on demand and sometimes, for example, around nap times, meal times, when tired and soon overnight, they are refused. This will make the protests at these times much worse. It is fairer on your baby and easier for you to move to feeding when offered.

To achieve this you need lots of activity, distractions, regular meals and snacks at the designated times, as well as water on offer. If you can, have others helping in the first couple of days. Then offer the feeds at the times they need the feeds.

Although daunting, many parents describe this as a bonding experience. You can learn other ways to comfort, entertain, relieve the boredom and play with your baby, which can be empowering for you and them. See this as a positive. Embrace it and the change will happen quickly.

POOR WEIGHT GAIN

I know how worrying this can be. My own baby, Henry, always struggled with weight gain. This was partly because he was naturally small, but also because milk made him uncomfortable due to severe reflux and an allergy to cows' milk protein. It makes you feel like you are failing. This is *not* the case at all.

Firstly, there is a huge difference between a small (low-weight) baby and a baby that's dropping weight. Take your baby's centile from what they were on at twelve to fourteen weeks. If your baby was on the 2nd percentile at twelve weeks and is still there now, they are **exactly** where they should be. There is no need to try to get them to eat more calories. They are taking what they need to maintain the weight they should be. It is ok for a baby to be naturally small.

If, however, your baby is dropping through the centiles and has dropped by more than 25 percent (since twelve weeks), there is usually a reason. This might be a short-term reason such as illness or teething, or they might be more mobile. Give them a couple of weeks after this stage has passed and your baby will catch up.

It could be medical, like Henry. Maybe baby can't keep milk down, is vomiting feeds, and is uncomfortable. CALM can work even if this is the case, and has helped lots of babies in this category. There are just some extra considerations. Please refer to the extra advice in the final chapter. I also encourage you to get baby weighed each month. The changes you make in the programme usually result in baby creeping back up the centiles.

Sometimes no reasons have been identified. If this is the case and you have already had baby looked over, or they are under the care of the GP or dietician[3], then proceed with the changes and I hope yours will be another success story, just like Megan's below.

> *This was more than just a sleep course for me, it was a lifeline. I don't have anyone to help or ask questions. I'm a first-time mum and was suffering with postpartum anxiety and found the sleep deprivation tough. Google was making everything worse and I was obsessing over the smallest things.*
>
> *Straight away Hannah gave us structure, which worked for me and my baby. She went from having lots of 5-minute feeds to 10-20-minute feeds and climbed a percentile.*

Fast forward five months, she sleeps through the night, has two naps a day, three meals a day, takes a bottle if needed, and I've recovered from postpartum anxiety! Me and my baby have the best relationship and she is thriving. I know it wouldn't be like this without Hannah's help. Thank you!

— MEGAN.

Note 3: As I am not supporting you, if your baby has any medical issues, including poor weight gain, it is vital that you are under the care of a GP or paediatrician and your baby is monitored through the process. My community details can be found in the final chapter and in the Sleep Well Hub. Please contact me if you require more support.

GENERAL NUTRITION TIPS, WHATEVER YOUR BABY'S AGE

There are key nutrition factors for all babies when following this programme. Please apply these at all your baby's meals.

Most importantly, **it does not matter how much your baby eats**. You need to be in control of what they are offered, at what times in the day, and where they eat. The rest should be left completely up to them. Whether they

eat or not is out of your control. The more you try
n to eat the less they will eat.

Secondly, **babies are very good at maintaining their calorie intake**. Your baby knows, even when you don't, that they don't need the extra calories you're trying to get them to eat. If your baby is following their growth line (from when they were twelve weeks) then they are getting exactly what they need. They do not need to eat more. If your baby feeds in the night, you need to actively reduce this to get them to eat more in the day. Don't expect your baby to suddenly eat more until you reduce the night-time milk.

Ensure all foods are high-calorie. Good foods to include are avocado, coconut milk and cream, nut butters, oily fish such as salmon, chicken thighs, twenty percent fat mince, eggs (especially the yolk), cheese, full-fat yoghurt, coconut yoghurt, hummus. You want every mouthful to count so avoid too many fruit and vegetables which contain few calories. This is especially important if you are reducing night-time feeds.

For the same reason, avoid pouches. Although there is nothing 'wrong' with pouches, they are low calorie, low protein, and low fat. These are the three things your baby needs right now. Pouches contain around four percent protein, whereas home-cooked meals can be up to forty percent protein. Your baby needs this protein to grow and develop – and to sleep. I won't ask you to cook gourmet meals three times a day. The meal ideas have been formulated to make things easy for you. Keep pouches to a minimum – or mix them with higher calorie foods like avocado, peanut butter or full-fat plain yoghurt when you do use them.

From a macronutrient point of view, there are two to focus on. The first is **protein,** as the body uses it to grow. Your baby is growing more than ever in this period. Therefore they need protein. Protein also keeps baby fuller for longer which is important when you want your baby to sleep well. Good protein foods are meat, fish, eggs, lentils, pulses, nut butter, hummus, dairy and legumes.

The second is fats. **Fats are so important at this stage.** Fats are high calorie and perform many vital functions in the body. All babies should have a high-fat diet. Good foods to include are avocado, olive oil, oily fish, coconut cream, eggs, dairy and nut butters.

Ensure you **keep fruit and vegetables to a maximum of five portions a day**. A portion fits into the palm of your baby's hand: one strawberry, two circles of banana or carrot, a small head of broccoli, six peas, or a fifth of an apple. Sometimes a baby is eating five or ten portions of one fruit as a snack – if they have half a banana or a bowl of strawberries.

Remember hydration, especially if your baby is reducing their milk feeds. **Offer water with all meals from a sippy cup**. This is the only fluid your baby should have other than milk, unless they are constipated and then you can offer a little prune juice.

Also **offer a variety, and combination, of finger foods and puree (or mashed).** Things like hummus, mashed avocado, porridge and yoghurt are easy to eat but finger foods keep your baby interested and are vital for hand-eye coordination, biting and chewing, and ensuring your baby isn't fussy. As you reduce overnight feeds your baby will need easy access to calories. If your baby prefers to be spoon-fed – go with it. If they prefer to feed themselves, that's ok too. All babies are different.

Keep milk feeds and meals separate. If your baby has milk near meal times, they won't learn that the food fills them up. This is especially the case if you feed milk alongside or after a meal. Feeding milk soon before meal times will mean your baby isn't hungry enough for the solids. Keep the two as separate as possible, as shown in the routines for each age.

Although you will reduce the frequency of feeding, don't limit your baby's milk intake in the day time. **If your baby finishes their daytime bottles always top them up.** There should always be twenty mls or more left in the bottle. They may well start to take more at each feed once they aren't feeding so frequently. Similarly, with breastfeeding, if they usually want just one side but start asking for the other, offer both. If, on the contrary, your baby isn't interested in a meal or milk feed then relax and let them decide. If it's a solid meal then keep it and if they seem hungry within the hour you can offer it to them again.

There is one medical issue that can occur with the increase in solids and that's constipation. **If your baby gets at all constipated,** stop all cereal and banana completely. Offer tinned or fresh prunes once a day. You can mix it with avocado or coconut cream for a pudding.

Also avoid using baby rice. This is milled white rice containing very little nutrition and can make babies constipated. Opt for a whole-grain baby cereal. One of the biggest causes of regular night-time waking in babies is constipation so do keep on top of this.

Many parents **worry about baby choking** on finger foods, but learning to manage lumps is important. At first, your baby might make terrible sounds, and some are even sick. This is them forming their gag reflex. Until your baby's gag reflex is formed, they are at a much higher risk of choking. The only way they can form their gag reflex is through practice. If your baby is making any sound at all they are not choking. Never leave a baby unattended when eating.

Finally, **portion sizes**. Your baby should be in control of this. Many parents say, "They ate half a portion of dinner," but if this is what they want to eat then *that is a full portion for them* – you just served double what they needed.

main points in mind so that weaning and food CALM process and your little one will form a ..g ..erm relationship with eating and sleep.

Weaning and feeding tips for all babies:

- It does not matter how much your baby eats.
- Babies are very good at maintaining their calorie intake.
- Ensure all foods are high-calorie.
- Avoid pouches.
- Focus on protein and fats.
- Limit fruit and vegetable portions.
- Offer water with all meals.
- Offer a variety, and combination, of finger foods and puree (or mashed).
- Keep milk feeds and meals separate.
- If your baby finishes their daytime bottles always top them up.
- If your baby gets at all constipated, stop cereal and banana completely

FUSSY EATING - PREVENTION AND CURE

Fussy eating is a common complication of poor sleep. A baby that feeds to sleep for naps, or uses the breast or bottle for comfort in the day and overnight will be harder to wean onto solids. Some babies do this and then eat well. If you have one of these babies watch out for their portions increasing and give easy access to calories through the high-calorie foods advised above.

If your baby is picky, their calories are variable, and you feel like you constantly need to 'persuade' them to eat, this can be frustrating and can contribute to your worry about reducing milk feeds for comfort, around nap times or overnight.

The first thing to know is that babies maintain their own calories very well, so we should relax and trust that. The more milk your baby or toddler drinks, the less food they will eat. This also goes the other way. As you reduce their milk they will naturally eat more food. Your baby or toddler will guide exact amounts, so you really don't need to worry.

THE BEST WAY TO TACKLE FUSSY EATING IS PREVENTION

I hate the term 'food before one is just for fun'. The first six months of weaning – between six and twelve months – is such a vital time. It is when they are open to new textures and flavours, and will try something they don't like again and again.

If you go by the 'food before one is just for fun' rule and don't encourage eating before twelve months, you aren't taking advantage of all the benefits the first six months of weaning give. Once baby is twelve months it is much harder to encourage them to try new foods, be open to new textures and flavours, and they definitely get fussier about trying things again and again, especially if they don't like it.

However, I agree that the best thing you can do to prevent fussy eating is make weaning fun. The more relaxed you are the more your baby will be too. The suggested routines of keeping milk and food separate will also help. The quicker your baby learns that food fills them up the quicker they will want the food when hungry. Another good tip to prevent fussiness is to reduce night-time milk as soon as is safe. Babies who feed more overnight need less food in the day and this can lead to fussiness.

Also ensure that you give attention to the behaviour you want (eating) rather than the not eating. All too often parents do the opposite and leave baby to it when they are eating. When they don't eat, that's when all the tricks come out: feeding; aeroplanes and trains; encouragement; distractions. Give lots of attention and praise when they are eating and ignore the non-eating. Either get on with your meal or take them down and offer later. Don't fall into the trap of offering alternatives, either. If your baby is offered yoghurt each time they refuse broccoli, they will soon learn to refuse broccoli. On this note, also ensure that you offer mainly savoury foods, especially at the start of weaning. Offering lots of sweet foods like yoghurt or even fruit will encourage a sweet tooth.

Finally, keep offering. Babies need to see and taste a certain food up to sixteen times to like and accept it. If your baby turns their nose up the first time, keep offering. Avoid hiding these foods in recipes, and move forward from puree. They need to learn what the food looks like and learn to like that food. The more foods you can get your baby to recognise and accept before they start walking – the time when the natural fussiness sets in – the better they will be at eating.

WHAT CAN YOU DO IF YOUR BABY IS ALREADY FUSSY?

Fussiness is a perfectly natural, albeit frustrating, stage all toddlers go through. There is a good reason for this stage: it is to protect them from accidental poisoning. As your little one starts to become more independent, is on the move, and can venture away from you, their natural instinct is to only eat what they recognise. Prior to this they are much more open to trying new flavours and eating foods they don't recognise. It is incredibly difficult to introduce your little one to new foods between the ages of two and four, which is why I recommend a varied diet before this time. The good news is that most babies will eat enough foods to remain healthy.

As an exercise, write down every food your baby will eat, has eaten recently and will occasionally take a bite of. They don't need to be their favourite foods, just ones they will sometimes accept. These are the foods you should start with.

It is also important not to overwhelm babies. This is especially important in older babies and toddlers. If they aren't very interested in eating, they can be put off by a huge portion. Keep their portion sizes small and then you can praise them when they finish… you can always offer more.

Ensure they are hungry at meal times. Cut out extra snacks and only offer milk at the daytime milk feed times in the routine. You will not see an increase in daytime feeds until the night-time feeds are addressed in module three.

For older toddlers, get them involved in cooking and choosing. Take them to the supermarket and make a meal plan that they help with. Toddlers love to know what to expect so these visual and 'away from the table' activities can help to alleviate their anxiety: cooking, baking, growing food, food play, messy play, drawing or colouring in can all help to normalise foods.

If you struggle with ideas, don't worry. You can find amazing recipes and meal ideas in your Sleep Well Hub. Follow the QR code to download these and your baby's routines.

DAYTIME CHANGES: PART THREE

YOUR SLEEP TECHNIQUE: HOW TO SETTLE YOUR BABY TO SLEEP IN THE NEW ROUTINE

MOVING FORWARD FROM YOUR SAFE PLACE AND HOW YOUR BABY WILL ADAPT

After all this feeding, weaning and routine preparation, you are finally ready to start the actual sleep training. I am not going to ask you to put your baby into their cot and walk away. As I promised, this is a gentle transition, but you do need a way of settling your baby to sleep that you can move forward from.

You read earlier about you and your baby's 'safe place' for sleep. You are now going to move forward from this. I will be explaining how we can make this possible. This is often a daunting step. It is perfectly normal to question if this first stage of the sleep training will work for you. Moving forward from what you view as your safe place is hard.

Every single person I have worked with on a one-to-one basis – and thousands who have followed my course or workshop – has managed this. That makes thousands of parents and babies since 2007. That isn't to say that some didn't find it hard, but it is usually much harder for the parent than the baby.

I can't overstress how vital it is for you to be confident in this process. Read the next chapter several times. When you finally implement this change, go into it knowing that it will work. Be confident and relaxed (and determined). How well you manage this directly correlates to how confident and relaxed your baby will be. If you are calm, consistent, and confident then your baby will be too.

Before you move on to possibly the most crucial part of the process – moving forward from your 'safe' place and taking the first step on your sleep tightrope towards your baby self-settling – here is a little recap.

You already have your baby's routine. You have a window for when the nap or bed time will happen. You have ways of checking if they are tired. You are also leading up to these times with lots of active play. You have your sleep triggers set and your room ready.

Now you are ready to get your baby to sleep. You will do this with your sleep technique.

THE SLEEP TECHNIQUE

Your new sleep technique is to lie down on the sleep mattress in your sleep room and cuddle your baby to sleep.

It doesn't matter how you hold your baby as long as you lie on the bed and you are comfortable. If you are already getting baby to sleep standing or sitting with a rock or pat, try to mimic this but while lying down. Include a bottom pat or hair stroke if that is what you already do.

There are video examples of this bed settling technique in your Sleep Well Hub: follow the QR code

It isn't important whether you choose a rock, pat, stroke or any other calming technique so long as you are consistent and don't swap between them all (remember the C of CALM is *consistent*). Choose one and stick to it. Your baby can adapt and learn this new way of settling. It is important to always hold baby in the same way. If others are helping and you are sharing the settles, you must all do the same technique. If one of you has baby on their right stroking their head and the other on their left patting, it is much harder to move forward because your baby is in effect going through two separate sleep training processes.

When getting your baby to sleep, *you* must be comfortable. A mum once called me when trying this for the first time. She had put a travel cot mattress on the baby's floor for the sleep space. She had no pillows and was trying to lie on this little mattress at the base of the cot, rocking baby in her arms. She was so uncomfortable – almost in pain from the technique. The baby was screaming and not settling. This mum's body language was awkward and uncomfortable, not a good message for the baby she was trying to settle. Babies are good at picking up on body language. For your baby to go to sleep they need to feel your confidence and comfort with this new situation. If they think you are awkward and uncomfortable, they will be too and will never go to sleep. The mum in question added some pillows and baby settled immediately once she was comfortable.

Practice this new settling to sleep technique for a minimum of one nap a day and to settle your baby for bed time too. Usually, the easiest nap to practise is the first morning nap: naps tend to get harder to instigate as the day gets later. I advise starting with this one and bring in other nap practice a couple of days into the programme.

If your baby is in childcare or not napping at home you can just practise at bed time, which can work, but you must ensure that bed times are perfect and you progress quickly to overnights (in the next module). If you don't practise naps, your baby will not be able to nap in their cot when you are home so, unless your baby is always at childcare and unable to practise there, I strongly advise practising nap times too.

YOUR NAP AND BEDTIME CHECKLIST

Have a little checklist in your head before starting any bed or nap time to minimise the chance of any settles not working. Firstly, assess tiredness. For this you can use the sleep signals, not being interested in playtime and the mirror and window trick.

Also think about the timings. If baby usually manages an hour and a half awake before first nap and seems tired after thirty minutes, be cautious about practising. Similarly, if you are doing second nap and the last wake window was an hour and a half yet baby now seems tired after forty-five minutes, offer some more food or play to check it isn't something else that is making baby grumpy. Offer a snack and some water **(not milk)** to ensure that they aren't hungry when going to sleep. This is especially important if they usually feed to sleep. Usually, awake windows increase as you go through the day.

Finally, know that quality is better than quantity when practising. It is better to practise one nap a day and always succeed than try to practise three naps a day and have only two work. Each 'failed' attempt affects your baby being able to go to sleep using the technique as they learn to cry rather than settle. For this reason, avoid naps after four pm using the technique. Go for a walk, have a cuddle (not in the sleep room), use the bouncer, or the car. Naps after four pm are much harder and often fail. Do ensure you practice at your baby's bed time though.

When you and baby are ready, do the final window and mirror check, the sleep triggers and then use the technique to settle.

Before you start the technique:

- Is baby tired? Think about routine timings as well as sleep signals.
- Could baby be hungry? Offer another snack if they might be (not milk).
- Have lots of active play. Only start when baby isn't interested in this play.
- Do not let baby relax at all leading up to nap or bed time.
- Check your baby is tired (window and mirror trick).
- Avoid naps after four pm using the technique.
- Remember, quality practice is better than quantity.
- Use your set sleep triggers.

HOW WILL MY BABY REACT TO THE TECHNIQUE?

When you settle your baby, they will behave in one of three ways. They may be upset, they may be angry, or they may mess around. The most important thing is your response *to* these behaviours.

The most common behaviour from your baby is anger. This is natural as they are tired and you are changing something. It is to be expected and unfortunately can't be avoided.

Anyone who says there is a 'no cry sleep solution' is lying. You never need to leave a baby to cry it out; you can be there to support and comfort them but all babies cry, especially with change. If your baby is angry their body language will be very different from the second most common reaction, upset – and your response to their behaviour should be very different too.

To illustrate the difference between anger and upset, let's take it away from a sleep situation. If your baby is upset because they have toppled over and banged their head or a stranger walks into the room, they will want cuddles; they will cling to you and want comfort, and their cry will be an upset cry. They will accept your help and comfort, and you will offer it.

If, however, your baby is cross – maybe you've taken your keys off them or you've refused your older baby a cereal bar just before a meal – their body language will be very different. They will not accept cuddles, will be back arching, and their cry will be a cross cry. They will not accept your help; they will push away. At this point you could give them the cereal bar or give the keys back and it would stop the situation immediately, but this isn't something you would do as you know this would encourage that behaviour in the future.

This is the same with sleep. If your baby is upset, crying, and accepting cuddles then you will offer them. You can comfort, help, and use the technique to settle your baby.

baby is back arching, pushing away, and is cross then you must listen to your baby and not encourage this behaviour by going back to what you were doing. When babies protest and refuse to settle, parents can often go backwards. Perhaps you start lying down, but they protest so you sit up. They still protest so you stand. They continue to protest so you hold them tighter, talk to them, bounce, walk around or feed. This is like giving the keys back, or the cereal bar, and encourages the escalation and the protests – exactly what you want to avoid.

If your baby doesn't accept help or cuddles, and is back arching and pushing away from you, continue with the technique as long as you feel comfortable. Give them a chance to settle to sleep. If you feel you can't continue, you **must do less**. This is where the cot comes into play. If your baby doesn't accept the cuddles, if they crawl away from you and are back arching, pop your baby into the cot. Sit down on the floor next to the cot and count to thirty very slowly in a very slow, calm and low voice. This will show your baby that you are calm and nothing is wrong.

When you reach thirty, if your baby is calmer in the cot than they were on the mattress, leave them longer. Count to fifty, one hundred, one hundred and fifty.

If they are more upset in the cot (or become upset when you count), after thirty seconds take them out and offer the technique on the mattress. Do not be tempted to cuddle standing up as you will make things so much worse when you lie down. The baby is either in the cot or on the nowhere else. **This is vital for the technique** If you are tempted to start cuddling sat up, to walk around with baby, to talk to them, or to have a quick cuddle as you go down to the mattress, don't. This will escalate the crying, and the programme will not work.

There is a third possibility, and that is they start messing around. Playing, poking you, laughing, rolling around, trying to crawl away (if they are mobile), thinking it is a game. Some amount of messing is ok. Once they are in their cot and you are out of the room, it doesn't matter how much they play around before they go to sleep. While you are there, it might be a little frustrating but soon that won't be the case. The rules surrounding this kind of behaviour depend on how much messing around there is. If they are just rolling around a bit, getting comfortable, let them continue. If they are hurting you, getting off the mattress, or it goes on for too long and they are not even trying to sleep, they must go into the cot the same as they would if they were protesting. If they still mess around in the cot, leave them until they ask to come out (by crying) but if you put them in and they are immediately upset, count to thirty and take them back to the mattress.

You **must** use the cot immediately if they do any of the following: hurt you, fight you, get off the mattress, anything dangerous, try to feed, crawl away, or aren't trying to sleep after five to ten mins.

The only thing to consider with extensive messing around is whether baby is tired enough. Typically, tired babies will go to sleep or protest. It is rare that a tired baby will want to play. If this happens frequently, increase awake windows, make sure there is no relaxing leading up to nap time, and assess tiredness.

Babies' reactions to the technique and how to help them:

1. **If they are upset:** *Indicated with upset crying but accepting cuddles*. Continue with the technique lying on the bed and cuddling. Support them, remain calm, focus on your breathing, and do not change what you are doing.
2. **If they are cross:** *Indicated by crying but not accepting cuddles, back arching, trying to get away, protest crying*. Continue as long as you can but if it gets too much, lift your baby gently and put them into the cot for thirty seconds. Sit back down at their level and count out loud to thirty very slowly and in a very low and quiet voice. 1....2.....3.....4......5... When you get to thirty, if they are more upset (screaming and crying), slowly get up and slowly lift them out and straight onto the mattress. No standing and cuddling or rocking. Continue with the same lying down technique. If they don't

accept the cuddles and help, put them back int the cot.

3. **Messing around, crawling off, playing:** Sometimes babies are just a bit confused – let your baby have a little play. They must stay on the mattress – if they crawl off, put them straight back into the cot. If they're just sitting, playing, lying down, let them get on with it. Stay with this unless they get upset (then cuddle – Point 1) or cross and crawl away (into cot and count – Point 2).

Remember – you either cuddle and do the technique, or your baby is in the cot and you are counting, or they are messing around on the mattress. ***Nothing else.***

The most important thing is to remain calm and act as if you have all the time in the world for your baby. Don't get stressed – it **will** work if you give it time and patience. The first settle typically takes twenty to thirty mins, and this very quickly reduces. By day three you might expect very few protests and your baby to settle well. Remember that you are there to offer help and support the whole time. The only time you 'do less' is if baby doesn't want that help or support.

Here are a few reminders and useful points when settling your baby to sleep:

- Never try to get your baby to sleep if they aren't tired. This will always get the biggest protests. They are just telling you 'I am not tired' – which is fair enough. How would you like someone to force you to sleep when you weren't tired?
- Try to have your mindset at 'I am here to support you when you are ready to sleep' rather than 'I am going to make you sleep'. Trying to make a baby sleep never works; allowing them support to sleep once they are ready does.
- If you are used to pushing your baby to sleep in the pram or feeding to sleep, the awake windows will be much bigger while learning to sleep by a different technique.
- Remember the window and the mirror trick. Wait until they are tired, and the protests will be much fewer. I would much rather have a baby playing happily for longer and a later bed or nap time, than a cross baby protesting for that extra half an hour because they aren't tired enough to sleep.
- To be able to judge tiredness you must ensure no relaxing or sleepy play leading up to bed or nap times.
- Your baby's awake times should increase as you go through the day, so the first awake time should be the shortest and the awake time before bed the longest.
- Finally, remember quality over quantity. If you are unsure about your baby's tiredness, you think they

might be ready to sleep but aren't sure, or the awake window is smaller than usual, opt for the pram or a car nap. Save the practice for when baby is definitely tired and you are confident you can succeed. Ensure this is a minimum of one nap a day and *every* bed time. Try to vary which naps you practise with too.

Once your baby is asleep you may leave them where they are on the mattress, or you can transfer them once completely asleep. There is no advantage to transferring. While baby is settling on the bed, they can sleep there and you can co-sleep with them. Once baby is self-settling in the cot that is where they will sleep. If you prefer to transfer them, wait until they are fully asleep before you make the transfer, and they are less likely to wake.

THE THREE CS: CALM, CONFIDENT AND CONSISTENT

Your baby will look to you to show them this new situation is ok, and they can relax and go to sleep. Your baby will not sleep without this reassurance.

The three Cs are paramount to the success of the settling technique. The settling technique succeeding is paramount to the success of the programme.

I cannot overstress the importance of these next few paragraphs.

C #1: CONSISTENT

The 'try everything' approach never works. If you aren't consistent with the changes, your baby will not have the chance to learn the new way to go to sleep. Consistency will reassure your baby. Each time you swap and change things, your baby will become confused about what is expected of them.

When learning something new you need to practise over and over. When learning to ride a bike or play an instrument it is practice that ensures you learn that new skill. That's what you are going to do with your baby: choose one technique and practise it over and over until it is the new normal. Then you can move forward again. In this way, you will take small steps towards your baby sleeping independently.

When you settle your baby choose one technique, one hold, one thing to help them. Avoid swapping and changing. Also ensure every person does the same thing: which side baby is being cuddled on, patting or rocking, where your hands are. The more consistent you are the easier it will be for your baby.

Another issue with an inconsistent approach is that you come across as nervous and, as you will see in the 'Calm' section below, it gets in the way of your baby learning this new way to go to sleep. When you are consistent, however, this also ensures you come across confident – the final C.

Consistency is especially important if you are not completely comfortable with the situation you are sleeping in. For example, you may find it harder to sleep on a flight than in your own bed.

Imagine you were trying to sleep on an aeroplane and were finding it difficult and the air hostess was swapping and changing what she was doing, opening the blind, closing it, turning on the air-con, turning it off, giving you a pillow, putting your footrest up, putting your chair back, and then up. You would *never* sleep. However, if she was just there, going about her business and allowing you a consistent environment to sleep in, you would be much more likely to sleep.

C #2: CALM

The one thing everyone needs to sleep – you, me, and your baby – is a calm environment. Babies are incredibly good at reading body language. If you go into the bedroom to get them to sleep in the new way and you are stressed, worried and tense, your baby will pick up this. I've seen this first hand on Zoom drop-in sessions in my Sleep Club. I see one parent pacing the room with a baby. When it comes to their turn to ask questions, they unmute and baby is screaming. They are obviously stressed: their voice is high and quick, their shoulders are up, and they are trying to settle baby with fast and vigorous bouncing.

I ask them to sit down and let me know in a very calm voice what's going on. Initially they find this impossible, but with a few words of encouragement they mimic my very slow, low and calm voice. The baby immediately stops crying. I continue to talk to the mum – about nothing really, just keeping them speaking – about their baby's routine, about weaning, about what they have on the rest of the day (they think it is relevant but it's not). They talk to me in a slow and low voice. After a little while I notice baby is asleep and I ask the mum how baby is. They are shocked to see that baby is fast asleep. Why? Because mum was relaxed. Gone was the vigorous bouncing, gone were the tight shoulders, the stressed voice, the 'need' to sleep.

There is not one person I know who would settle in a situation that isn't calm.

Your baby looks to you for reassurance. If you were on a plane and hated turbulence and the plane started bobbing up and down, you would look to the air hostess. If they are calm and happy, continuing with their work, this reassures you. If they were strapping in and looking nervous, this would exacerbate your anxiety. Show your baby everything is ok.

Here is another scenario that illustrates the importance of being calm.

When I was a student nurse working night shifts in the hospital, there were often screaming babies whose parents were not able to get them to sleep. The parents were understandably stressed: their baby was sick, they were in hospital, and the baby was screaming and keeping everyone awake – who wouldn't be stressed? This is where I first started my 'sleep techniques'. When I had a moment, I would go over to them and offer to take their baby so they could go and have a coffee or get some fresh air. Within minutes their baby was asleep on me. Why? Because I was calm. The baby could sense it and then relaxed and went to sleep.

C #3: CONFIDENT

When you are confident, you will be calm and consistent. Having the confidence that you and your baby are ok will mean you succeed. Go into that room with confident body language, be consistent with the change, and show your baby you can do this. Your baby will look to you for reassurance and if you show them this is possible, they will adapt to the change.

Imagine someone trying to get you to do something unusual for you, like a skydive. If they were unsure about it, nervous, not confident in themselves or the parachute, if they were hesitant, getting upset, changing what they were doing, or asking for help… there is *no way* you would jump out of the plane. If, however, your instructor was confident and sure it was going to work, was consistent with their advice, and supported you the whole time, you would be much more likely to put your confidence in them and jump out of that aeroplane. You need to be that confident instructor for your baby throughout the whole process.

The three Cs are the cornerstone principles to **every stage** of the process. Read them again at every change you make, as they are the key to the success of each stage.

MODULE TWO SUMMARY

There's a lot of information in this module, which I appreciate can be overwhelming. Some people want the bare minimum in simple instructions, while others want to know exactly why and how and all the background. If you are the former type of person, here are the areas to focus on to achieve module two:

- Aim for the timings on the routine for your baby's age; ensure milk feeds, meals and sleeps are separate.
- Focus on high-calorie foods; fats and protein are the most important food groups.
- Move away from feeding on demand; only let your baby feed when you offer.
- Have sleep triggers as a part of your naptime and bedtime routine; the triggers should be the same for naps and night time and the same whoever is putting baby to bed; milk feeds should be separate, and well away from naps and bed time.
- Practise the new settling technique for a minimum of one nap and bed time every day from the start of the training; follow the three Cs and 'do less' if baby

is protesting; remember your body language and slow counting (with baby in the cot) if they aren't settling to sleep.

- Make sure baby is tired; use the window and mirror trick and lots of active play leading up to nap and bed times.
- Practise this technique until it becomes easier and you are confident it will work for you each time (even if there is still some crying).

> *"Before we started we felt at breaking point. With a return to work looming, long bed times of rocking to sleep and around ten wake ups a night, we'd had serious discussions around whether I could go back, which wasn't an option for us. Something had to change. We liked Hannah's gentle approach, but being honest, both felt quite sceptical about whether her technique would work with our extremely active ten-month-old. After a tough first bed time we were still filled with doubt, but within three days he was going to sleep in under five minutes with no crying and only three wake ups a night.*
>
> *At the end of week one, we're completely mind-blown about where we are already and are now looking forward to progressing further rather than dreading making changes. We absolutely could not have got to this point without Hannah's advice!"*
>
> — EMMA BEASLEY

CHECKLIST: are you ready for module three?

Before moving to the next module *(Night-time Changes)* are the following true?

- The technique is working well for bed time and nap time. There might still be protests but you are confident your baby will go to sleep.
- You are practising a variety of naps if your baby naps more than once.
- Sleeps and feeds are separated in the day, including at bed time.
- Milk feeds and solid feeds are separated.
- You have been consistent with sleep triggers and your baby knows them.

The above takes between five and ten days in most babies.

---

1. *This natural improvement is typically seen in about 75% of my sleep programmes. Some parents don't see improvement in the night-time changes until they start to tackle them. If you find this is the case for you then progress to the night-time changes more quickly – these are all found in module three – but not before you complete the daytime changes.*
2. *This is taken from bed time, irrespective of overnight wakes or feeds so an 8 pm bed time means a 6 am wake up.*
3. As I am not supporting you, if your baby has any medical issues, including poor weight gain, it is vital that you are under the care of a

GP or paediatrician and your baby is monitored through the process. My community details can be found in the final chapter and in the Sleep Well Hub. Please contact me if you require more support.

MODULE THREE: NIGHT-TIME CHANGES

A NOTE ABOUT MODULES THREE AND FOUR

Although I am insistent that people do not jump ahead, there can be some interchanging between module three (the night-time changes) and module four (the sleep training). If you feel super confident with your settling technique, you can start working through the sleep training stages as outlined in module four alongside the night-time changes in module three.

Moving forward can help with the night-time changes. As your baby becomes more confident and independent at settling, they will find it easier to re-settle at night. Do ensure that you move forward in both the night time and day time, not only in the day. You don't want to be at the stage of walking out the room for naps and bed time, and still mattress settling overnight, for example.

In module two you practised the settling technique to get your baby to sleep. Now you are going to use that technique to help your baby re-settle after their overnight wakes.

REDUCING NIGHT-TIME FEEDS: INTRODUCTION

The worst thing about night-time feed reductions is the confusing and conflicting advice. Parents are told their baby 'doesn't need night feeds so just stop offering' and the opposite, that 'babies need milk overnight until twelve or even eighteen months so you must continue to feed if they ask'. Neither extreme is true.

If your baby feeds in the night, they will take fewer calories in the day time to compensate (remember, your baby is extremely good at maintaining their own calorie intake). Therefore, they 'need' the overnight calories the next night to compensate in turn. However, you can reverse this nocturnal eating and get baby taking all the calories they need in the day time. This is one of the most rewarding parts of any sleep programme: if you have a baby who is uninterested in daytime feeds, not weaning onto solids well or only having a couple of ounces of milk at a time, once you reduce the night-time feeds, they suddenly start eating more. You no longer need to lock yourself away in a dark room to feed and your lovingly prepared foods are eaten rather than thrown on the floor.

Despite this, parents often feel nervous about this step. They think they will be starving their baby, that baby won't take more calories in the day time, and they are refusing them the milk they need. To reassure you, babies naturally need less milk in the night as they get older. It is not unusual for a baby to take one to two night feeds at two months old and 'need' five or more by the time they are seven months. They do not need these extra night-time feeds.

You can find further reassurance in how hungry baby is in the morning. If your baby wakes in the morning and will wait for their morning milk, or is not really interested, or takes only a small amount, this is a telling sign that they are having more milk in the night than they in fact 'need'.

Reducing night-time feeds can be difficult, not only because it's a convenient and easy way to re-settle your baby, but because in the middle of the night crying seems to be elevated by twenty decibels. On top of this, your ability to remain calm, consistent and confident at this time often goes out of the window.

I am going to stress again, above anything else, the importance of the three Cs and how vital they are when addressing and removing the night-time feeds. As you have experienced in the day time, your baby will adapt if you are calm, confident and consistent. I want to you use the experience of your baby adapting in the day to increase your capability to be calm, confident and consistent overnight too.

IF YOU ARE FEEDING ONLY ONCE OVERNIGHT, OR NOT AT ALL:

If you are only feeding once overnight, or not at all, all you need to do is master the lying down technique for all other wakes. Because this technique is outside of the cot, it is fine for you to continue to co-sleep and not transfer baby back to the cot. If you feel more confident using the technique and then transferring, ensure baby is fully asleep before the transfer.

If your baby is used to being settled in the night by rocking standing up (for example), they might find this stage hard. Be consistent, calm and confident, just as you have been in the day time, and they will adapt. Also use the cot, and counting, if they protest or do not settle. Apply all the same things you have done in the day time and it'll work.

Once you have mastered this and baby settles using the mattress technique at every night-time wake (apart from the one possible feed), you can move to module four.

However, if your baby feeds more than once in the night you need to tackle the other feeds…

SETTLING YOUR BABY OVERNIGHT *WITH* A FEED

There are times in the night to feed your baby, and times to settle them without feeding. If your baby wakes at a time when they are due a feed, feed them as soon as you go to them. It is so important not to try to get your baby to go to sleep first and then end up feeding them. Lift them as soon as you go to them, feed them, and then put them back down. If they fall asleep feeding that's fine; if they don't you can use the technique to settle them back off.

SETTLING YOUR BABY OVERNIGHT *WITHOUT* FEEDING

The biggest reason for increased crying overnight and the programme not working is if you try to settle without feeding and then resort to feeding. This encourages the crying and discourages the settling. You can take small steps, so you can be confident to settle your baby should they wake before the time you are allowed to feed.

At the times you are settling your baby without feeding, go to your baby and check they are ok, and you can reassure them with a cuddle. If they are very sleepy, it is fine to go straight to the technique. If they seem more awake, or upset, then assess how tired they are. If they seem 'awake' (if you wouldn't be trying to get them to sleep in the day time), wait until they are tired. You may do this in your arms but avoid holding them in a position they could get sleepy in. You could hold them on the end of your knee or lie them in the cot, or on the mattress, with some music or a light show. Once they are ready to go to sleep, showing sleep signals and uninterested in being awake, use the technique to get them back to sleep, just as you have practised in the day.

When settling your baby, absolutely ensure the three Cs and remember to do less if your baby protests, otherwise it won't work. Remember you can swap over with someone is supporting if you need to and you have that option.

The most important thing is not to give in and feed after you have started settling without. Continue with the technique. If it gets too much, use the cot for the thirty-second count. Worse case, have a break, sit up and check baby is ok, then re-set. Once tired, go back to the technique.

The first time might take a while. The first couple of settles can be hard, just like the first time you settle in the day time with the technique. You may well feel this is ridiculous as you know feeding would get baby off quickly and now you're awake longer, but this is for a reason. To get your baby sleeping well you must push past this stage.

As your baby adapts, you'll see they quickly realise they can settle without feeding at night, just as they have been in the day. The time it takes to settle reduces quickly.

Re-settling without feeding in the night:

- Go in and check ok.
- Quick cuddle to assess tiredness.

- If too awake, hold baby in an awake position until tired (for example, the end of your knee sitting on a chair).
- Once ready to sleep, repeat some sleep triggers (sentence, music) and go to technique.
- Settle with technique.
- Remember three Cs and use the cot if needed.
- You can co-sleep or transfer once asleep.
- There is no advantage to not co-sleeping at this point.

MORE AWAKE TIME IN THE NIGHT?

When you first settle baby without feeding in the night this can result in your baby being awake for longer periods. This is natural for anyone, even you. If you wake in the night for a quick toilet visit you'll get back into bed and go straight to sleep; this is the equivalent for your baby to waking for a feed. If you wake up with a startle, maybe because of a loud noise, you will feel different as it isn't 'normal' for you. You will suddenly be awake and alert to find out what the noise was. By the time you realise it's just a picture that's fallen off the wall and you get back into bed, it takes you an hour to get back to sleep again. This is because it's different; something has changed, the hormones start going and you can't get back to sleep. It is the same for your baby.

Baby wakes up, expecting the feed. By the time you've refused it and started doing the technique, they have woken up too much, the hormones have started going around and this prevents them from going to sleep again. They're just too awake. Soon the technique will be normal for their overnight wakes and they will go back to sleep very easily, just like you do when you get up to go to the toilet.

WHEN TO FEED AND WHEN NOT TO FEED?

Starting with the first part of the night, you will put in manageable gaps. This is the easiest part of the night to settle baby without feeding. This first manageable gap will be from bed time to midnight – typically the longest stretch in any twenty-four-hour period a baby can manage to not feed. It should be perfectly manageable for your baby to go through from bed time until midnight. Some babies will do this naturally because of the daytime changes, or even before this. If your baby is, that's great… you've achieved this part of the process. If not, follow the non-feeding steps in the section above to settle your baby to sleep without feeding between bed time and midnight.

If your baby feeds many times during this period you might take a few days to achieve this. Focus on the first wake up, even if you end up feeding a couple of times before midnight. It shouldn't take longer than a few days to achieve this four- to five-hour goal.

The aim is to get to midnight and then have one big feed on the first wake up after twelve. This can be as much as your baby wants to take from the breast or bottle.

After this one post-midnight feed, it is fine to keep feeding as you always have, but try to keep them short or small, ideally half the length or amount of your baby's daytime feeds. If they aren't asleep at this point, use the technique to settle back off. Lift them up and give them a cuddle when you take them off the bottle or breast if you need to, until they are calm. Then pop them down and settle using the technique.

Here is an example of how your night might look at the end of this initial stage:

7.30 feed and play after
8 pm bed with technique
9.30 baby wakes and settle with technique
11.30 baby wakes and settle with technique
12.45 baby wakes and settle with a feed (30 mins on breast or 6oz bottle)
2.30baby wakes and you feed (kept to 10 mins/3oz)
3.30 baby wakes and you feed (10 mins/3oz)
5 am baby wakes and you feed (10 mins/3oz)
6.30 baby wakes and you start the day – feed offered 1oz taken
Once you've managed this first gap, you can focus on some more of the night.

SECOND PART OF THE NIGHT: MIDNIGHT – 4 AM (AND ON TO MORNING)

Once baby is not feeding between bed time and twelve, focus on the next part of the night. Encourage another three-hour gap after baby's big post-midnight feed, and further reduce the other feeds.

Building on the above example, this might look like this:

> 7.30 feed and play after
> 8 pm bed with technique
> 9.30 baby wakes and you settle with technique (should be easier by now)
> 11.30baby wakes and you settle with technique
> 12.45 baby wakes and you offer big feed (30 mins on breast or 6oz bottle)
> 2.30 baby wakes and you settle with the technique
> 3.50 baby wakes and you feed (7 mins/2oz)
> 5 am baby wakes and you feed (7 mins/2oz)
> 6.30 baby wakes and you start the day – feed offered 3oz taken

Then you can increase to a four-hour second gap after the midnight feed, and also push that feed to after one am:

> 8 pm bed with technique
> 11.30 baby wakes and you settle with technique
> 12.45 baby wakes and you settle with technique

1.30 baby wakes and offer big feed
3.40 baby wakes and self-settles (you might see this more as you continue)
4.40 baby wakes and you offer small feed (5 mins/2oz)
6.30 baby wake and you start the day – feed offered 4oz taken

Remember these are just examples. It is impossible to predict when babies will wake or how many times. Your baby may have nights when they wake only a couple of times, and then a few nights waking ten times. Please try to avoid looking into this too much. Night-time wakes vary – this is why you need to get to the point of your baby settling without feeding. Once this is achieved, you can move through the sleep training and get to self-settling. Once your baby self-settles at night they will still wake as many times but will be able to re-settle themselves. You may see them shuffle about, move around, re-position themselves, and maybe even cry out, but they won't need you.

The important thing is that you slowly increase the gaps between feeds, and slowly reduce the amount they take.

IF YOU ARE COMBINATION FEEDING

If you are combination feeding, mums often breastfeed in the night. Understandably, it's much easier than making up bottles. If this is you, start the reduction in the breastfeeding, and get down to two feeds. If you get a little stuck at this point you might find it easier to swap to a bottle for the final part. This removes some of the comfort and you can see exactly how much your baby is taking.

If you do this, go in, lift baby and offer the bottle. If they take it, great. If not, pop them back down. You might lift and offer two or three more times. If your baby is hungry, they will take it. If they don't take it, settle with the technique. Avoid offering the breast if your baby refuses the bottle.

MORE ABOUT MILK, NUTRITION AND FOOD, IN RELATION TO NIGHT-TIME CHANGES

As you reduce the night-time feeds your baby will naturally compensate for the drop in calories overnight by taking more calories in the day. This will be from milk as well as food, if weaned. Your baby is getting enough milk if there is 1oz left in all their daytime bottles once they have finished feeding. If they finish the whole bottle, top it up. If breastfeeding, your baby may want to feed for longer, or from both breasts. If your baby is older than seven months, has fewer than four daytime feeds, and seems hungry, you could temporarily increase daytime feeds to be in line with the seven-month routine. Go back to the routine for their age as soon as you have tackled the night-time feeds.

The above instructions are a guideline. As long as you are increasing the time between feeds and reducing time on the breast overnight, it is working. In a bottle-fed baby you can note the amount of night-time milk and know it is reducing. On breast-fed babies you can often tell if your breasts feel full overnight. This is a good indication that your baby is taking less milk. You will soon adapt and be more comfortable; try to avoid expressing as this will increase milk production while you want to reduce it overnight.

Usually, the easiest part of the night is bed time to first feed. If you find this tricky, look at the end of your baby's day. Ensure a good gap between afternoon milk and dinner, and a minimum two-hour gap between finishing dinner and bedtime milk. Also, make sure bed time isn't before eight pm.

At this point in the programme, nutritionally speaking, focus on high-calorie and high-fat foods in the day time. Include avocado, coconut cream, full fat yoghurt, hummus (add extra olive oil), salmon, chicken thighs, tuna and salmon mayonnaise, egg yolk, cheese, cream cheese, peanut butter, cashew nut butter, and smoothies made with coconut cream, fruit, avocado and nut butter. Also keep fruit, vegetables and pouches to a minimum and remember to offer water at meal times – the reduction in feeds also means a reduction in fluids. Finally, remember your baby will take what they need and they adapt quickly so try to have faith in their ability to maintain their calories.

MOVING FORWARD TO MODULE FOUR

I haven't given a checklist for you to 'pass' this module as you can absolutely move forward through the stages in module four while you address night-time feeds. The only thing I would like to highlight is that you must get down to one feed as soon as possible. This is a huge turning point for most families I work with. If you are struggling, getting to that point makes things so much easier and less complicated. Avoid stalling on more than one feed for long: on my one-to-one programmes I aim for families to be down to a single feed within ten days of starting, no matter their situation.

While your baby is settling on the bed with you, it is fine to co-sleep. In fact, it is better to co-sleep and feed less than try to transfer baby to the cot and they wake up more for feeds.

MODULE FOUR: THE SLEEP TRAINING

GENTLY REMOVING YOU FROM YOUR BABY'S SLEEP PROCESS AND TEACHING THEM TO SLEEP INDEPENDENTLY

YOUR TECHNIQUE

In module two you read about the lying down technique to settle your baby for naps and bed time. In module three you used this same technique to eliminate night-time feeds and settle for night-time wakes. In this module you will move forward from this lying down technique, using a number of stages to get to self-settling. At each stage your baby will do more to help themselves sleep and you will do a little less, until your baby doesn't rely on you at all to settle and sleeps independently.

You can perfect the technique in 'stages'. As you follow each stage your baby will rely on you less and less. In these small steps you will achieve your baby sleeping independently.

When you move forward your baby will initially protest a little more but, as you have already seen in the initial stage, they soon adapt and this becomes their new normal. Once they have adapted you can move forward again.

WHEN TO MOVE FORWARD?

There are bigger stages such as cot settling, and small steps like reducing the patting, so there may be some variation. Cot settling might last four days while your baby adapts, whereas reducing the patting might only take twenty-four hours.

I advise *no more* than four days at each stage, just long enough for them to adapt to the change, but not enough time for them to build new habits. Stalling at a stage can often mean more protests – both at that stage and when moving forward.

I am often asked if baby needs to not be crying at all before moving forward. This isn't vital: some babies do have a cry before settling; this is their grumpiest part of the day and if they are tired and grumpy they might well cry. Some babies even cry at the anticipation – when you walk upstairs or put their sleepsuit on. As long as they do go to sleep, this isn't a reason not to move forward.

As a guide, get to cot settling within two weeks of starting the programme. From that to walking out should not take longer than a further two weeks.

I can't overstress how important it is to keep moving forward. Stalling at one stage is the biggest reason for regressions.

KEY THINGS TO REMEMBER WHEN MOVING FORWARD

There are some key things to remember at each stage, and these will help your baby settle well and quickly. First and foremost, remain calm. Your baby needs you to show them that each stage is ok. Remember your body language, breathing, and slow body movements to show your baby that this is ok.

Secondly, be consistent. Choose one rate for the patting or rubbing; hold the same hand on your baby. Once you get to cot settling, stand or sit in the same position, never swap and change. This will reassure your baby. It is vital you always 'do less' if your baby protests (more on this below).

Also remember, once you move forward don't ever go back as this will encourage more protesting. Forget the last technique you did so you're not tempted to go back if your baby protests.

Finally, it's fine for your baby to mess around a little, either getting comfortable or playing. If they do this, just sit next to them and wait until they're ready to sleep. Then you can help them.

Here is another air hostess scenario.

If you hate turbulence and the plane starts to jump up and down, the first thing you do is look to the air hostess. If she is relaxed and continuing to do her job, you will relax too. If she is strapping in, looking worried, you will also worry more. Your baby, at each stage, looks to you for reassurance. If you are able to relax, your baby will too. If your body language is worried, baby will pick up on that.

Be that confident air hostess and show your baby this change is ok.

At each stage:

- Remain calm.
- Be consistent.
- Be confident in the change.
- Always 'do less' if your baby protests.
- Once you move forward don't go back.
- It is fine for your baby to mess around a little.

YOUR SLEEP TRAINING STAGES

Detailed below are the steps to achieve your baby sleeping independently. A table also summarises these steps. It is absolutely vital you 'do less' at each stage. This is what reduces the protests in the long run (even if they escalate initially). You don't have to implement every step. Parents often skip some of the smaller steps but if you genuinely want to make very gradual changes these are all the stages you need.

STAGE 1: LYING DOWN, CUDDLING AND ROCKING (YOU CAN SEE THIS IN YOUR SLEEP WELL HUB)

For this technique you lie on your mattress, on your side. Cuddle your baby into you. The usual position is tummy to tummy with their head on your arm while you rock your baby using your hand or your body.

Common adaptions: you might pat your baby's bottom or back. Some parents have baby facing outwards, 'spooning' them. This can be the case if Mum usually feeds lying down.

Tips: ensure you and baby are comfortable. Use cushions to support you. If you aren't comfortable, baby will notice the tension. Hold baby tightly to make sure they feel comforted and supported. If you rock or pat do so slowly. This will mean you come across calmly. If you rock fast or pat quickly you can seem stressed. Choose one rate (perhaps one rock per second) and stick to that.

Doing less: if baby is upset, continue with the technique as long as you feel comfortable. Remember to remain calm, consistent and confident. Remember your body language, slow breathing and don't adapt what you are doing. If baby is back arching and trying to get away, or it gets too much, then slowly lift baby into the cot, sit next to the cot and count to thirty out loud in a very low and slow voice. If baby is angrier or more upset in the cot, after thirty seconds lift slowly back out and straight onto the mattress. Avoid any cuddles on the way down. If baby is less upset in the cot, continue counting until they 'ask' to come out (start crying).

It is very normal for baby to be more upset initially in the cot. In fact, that is what you want. Do not let that put you off using the cot. You want baby to not want to be in the cot initially so that they accept being on the mattress. As you use the cot more, they will get used to it and be less upset. If baby is ever happier in the cot, leave them there longer. Carry on counting. The more you use the cot in the early stages, the easier cot settling will be when you get to it.

STAGE 2: LYING DOWN, CUDDLING BUT OFF YOUR ARM (SO YOUR ARM IS OVER THE TOP OF YOUR BABY'S HEAD) AND PATTING THEM

For this technique you lie on your mattress, on your side. Cuddle your baby into you. The usual position is tummy to tummy with your arm over their head so their whole body and head are on the mattress. Rock or pat your baby using your hand or your body.

Common adaptions: you might pat your baby's bottom or back. Some parents have baby facing outwards, 'spooning' them but their whole body must be on the mattress, including their head.

Tips: same as stage one.

Doing less: Same as stage one.

STAGE 3: LYING DOWN WITH A GAP BETWEEN YOU AND YOUR BABY, STILL PATTING THEM BUT AT ARM'S LENGTH

For this technique you lie on your mattress, on your side with your baby next to you but with a gap. You can still touch them with your hands but they are at least ten cm away from you.

Common adaptions: you might pat your baby's bottom or back. Some babies might be on their tummy or side (if able to get there themselves).

Tips: it is common for baby to roll into you or try to crawl on you. Move them away, gently, once. If they continue to roll into you, it is time to use the cot. Do not be frightened to use the cot. The more you use it at this stage, the easier cot settling will be. If baby is crawling around the cot, leave them there longer. Be very consistent with never letting baby cuddle in.

Doing less: Same as stage one but use the cot as soon as baby tries to cuddle in or doesn't stay with a gap between you.

STAGE 4: SAME AS STAGE THREE BUT WITH YOU SITTING UP

For this technique you sit up on the mattress with your baby next to you, with a gap. You can still touch them with your hands but they are at least ten cm away from you.

Common adaptions: many parents skip this step and go straight to cot settling.

Tips: if baby is relentless with rolling next to you in stage three, you might want to do this instead as it means you can't cuddle into your baby. If you do both stage three and four, only do this one for twenty-four hours. It is a stepping stone.

Doing less: same as stage one but use the cot as soon as baby tries to cuddle in or doesn't stay with a gap between you.

Important note: The more you use the cot in these final 'out of the cot' stages, the easier your baby will find the cot transition. Start to become 'stricter' with using the cot for counting. If baby doesn't settle, pop them into the cot. It is he babies that haven't been in and out of the cot ho find cot settling much harder.

STAGE 5: COT SETTLING

For this technique you keep all the same timings and sleep triggers, and remember the three Cs. Instead of settling baby on the mattress, settle them in the cot. Use the same technique you have been doing on the mattress (patting/ rocking).

Common adaptions: try not to adapt *anything*: keep the same side of your baby, the same hand hold, same patting, same consistency. The difference is that baby is in the cot and you are next to the cot.

Tips: it is common for babies to mess around a lot, expect to be taken out the cot (never do this), and take longer to settle. This is the final 'big' stage: it's all downhill from here. Remain calm, be there for your baby, offer the technique and they will accept it. It is fine to put your baby back into their sleep position a few times, even put some slightly firm pressure on them to stay there, but otherwise sit next to the cot (it is often better to be at their level) and wait until they are ready to accept your help to sleep. Always 'do less' if they are screaming, protesting, or not settling.

Doing less: once your baby is cot settling, 'doing less' means moving away from the cot and counting. At this stage just move a small distance away, turn your back, stop offering help and slowly count to thirty. If baby is less upset, stay away; if baby is more upset, go back to the cot. At this point, attempt to put baby into their sleep position and offer the technique to sleep. Some parents do this all at floor level, while some stand.

STAGES 6-8: REDUCING THE PATTING/ROCKING

For this technique you gradually reduce the patting or rocking to get to the point of holding your hand still on your baby. You can do this by reducing the rock or pat every twenty-four hours, initially to one rock or pat every second, then reduce to one every 2 seconds and then down to every four seconds. After this just hold your hand still.

Common adaptions: Many parents skip these steps and move to holding their hands still. Start leaving the door of the sleep room ajar at this stage so that the final stages are easier.

Tips: never go backwards. Do not pat more if baby cries more, even though it is very tempting. Always do less and step back if baby protests at the reduced movement.

Doing less: same as stage five, step back, turn around and count.

STAGE 9: HOLDING YOUR HAND STILL ON BABY

For this technique you stand in the same position and have a still, light hand on your baby.

Common adaptions: you might hover your hand above baby to help with the next stage.

Tips: never go backwards. Do not hold your hand more firmly or start moving it once you have moved to hands still. If baby sits or stands up, always move away and 'do less'.

Doing less: move further away than the previous stage. Whether you are at floor level or standing, move halfway between the cot and door to count.

STAGE 10: STANDING NEXT TO THE COT

For this technique you put baby into the cot, leave your hand on for five seconds, then stand or sit next to the cot in the same position but not touching your baby.

Common adaptions: if you have an older baby, at this point they might take to a comforter, especially if they have been holding your arm or hand in the cot. If they find it hard, wrap the comforter around your hand initially.

Tips: always do less if baby protests. Don't be tempted to go back to holding your hand on them for longer than five seconds.

Doing less: move further away. Whether you are at floor level or standing, move to the doorway with the door ajar to count.

STAGE 11: STANDING IN THE MIDDLE OF THE ROOM

For this technique you put baby into the cot, leave your hand on for five seconds, then stand or sit in the middle of the room, halfway between the cot and the door.

Common adaptions: you might still be sitting on the floor. If so you might want to stand at this point.

Tips: always do less if baby protests. Don't move closer. Leave the room if protesting. Practise going in and out of the room and leaving your baby in their awake hours when they are playing – if you need to go to the toilet, when you put washing on, or when you make lunch. Leave them somewhere safe and get them used to you leaving and returning. This will help.

Doing less: at this point, leave the room. Parents who practise leaving the room and returning more at this stage and the next have babies that adapt to waking up well. Do not go back in if baby is ok when you leave, only if baby is upset without you there. Never shut the door.

STAGE 12: STANDING IN THE DOORWAY

For this technique you put baby into the cot, leave your hand on for five seconds and then stand in the doorway with the door ajar.

Common adaptions: it is often the case that you leave the room and baby is ok. If you leave (to do less) and baby is ok, **don't come back in.** This is often a natural move to walking out.

Tips: always do less if baby protests. Don't move closer. Leave the room if protesting. Practise going in and out of the room and leaving your baby in their awake hours when they are playing – if you need to go to the toilet, when you put washing on, or when you make lunch. Leave them somewhere safe and get them used to you leaving and returning. This will help.

Doing less: As stage eleven.

STAGE 13: WALKING OUT!

For this technique you put baby into the cot, leave your hand on for five seconds and then walk away, leaving the door open in case you need to go back.

Common adaptions: Many parents stay close, out of sight. Don't! Leave: walk away, give yourself a job, avoid hanging around. This must become normal for both of you.

Tips: This is very different from controlled crying. Module five explains the big difference between this programme and controlled crying.

Doing less: stay away… but if you need to pop back, just walk in calmly, lie baby into sleep position, leave your hand on for five seconds and then go again. Avoid being in the room for any longer than this.

Stage	Sleep training stage	How to do less
1	Lie down, cuddle and pat (video from your Sleep Well Hub, described in module two)	Into cot and count slowly (out loud) for thirty seconds
2	Lie down and cuddle but off your arm (so your arm is over the top of your baby's head), patting	Into cot and count slowly for thirty seconds
3	Lie down with a gap between you and your baby, patting	Into cot and count slowly for thirty seconds
4	Sit up next to your baby on the bed and pat them	Into cot and count slowly for thirty seconds
5	Settle in the cot with the patting technique	Stop patting. Take your hand away, leaving baby in the cot. Turn around and count slowly for thirty seconds
6	Slow the pat to one every second	Stop patting and count slowly for thirty seconds
7	Slow the pat to one every two seconds	Stop patting and count slowly for thirty seconds
8	Slow the pat to one every four seconds	Stop patting and count slowly for thirty seconds
9	Stop patting and hold your hand still	Take your hand away and count
10	Put your hand on baby for five seconds. Take it away and replace a max of every minute for five seconds if they need you to	Move away from the cot. Walk towards the door and count slowly for thirty seconds
11	Put your hand on baby for five seconds. Take it away and move halfway to the bedroom door. If you need to replace your hand you can, after you have done less, but then move back again	Leave the room. Stand outside the door with the door open and count slowly for thirty seconds. When you go back in you may put baby back into their sleep position and then go back to the door
12	Put your hand on baby for five seconds. Take it away and move to stand in the doorway. If you need to replace your hand, you can, after you have done less, but then move back again	Leave the room. No counting out loud (count in your head). When you go back in you can put baby back into their sleep position and then go back to the door
13	Put your hand on baby for five seconds. Take it away and leave the room	If you need to go back in, do - a max of every one to five minutes. Check they're OK, put them into their sleep position and leave

WHEN TO 'DO LESS'

There is a big difference between a baby that is protesting and a baby that is just winding down. You want your baby to be able to be in their cot and do their wind down before falling asleep in there. That means they might sometimes go in and play, whinge, or mess around for a while before falling asleep.

If your baby is messing around on the mattress, sitting up, flopping back down, bottom in the air, and rolling, or standing once in the cot, cruising around the cot chatting, or playing with comfort toys, just sit next to them on the mattress or next to the cot. At this point don't 'help' them, but there is no need to move away. Be there and wait for them to be ready to sleep. You could play on your phone or read or even pretend you're asleep.

But when your baby is protesting, fighting it, screaming, standing and generally demanding you or your attention – *this* is when you 'do less'. This is when you step back.

If your baby thinks it is play time each time you start the technique and takes a long time to settle, you might want to assess whether you're judging tiredness correctly, using the window and mirror trick. If you know they are tired but they still mess around a lot, leaving the room and coming back can help (leaving them in the cot). Sometimes babies need to realise staying up isn't fun any more so don't be frightened of 'doing less' if they are just messing around.

Remember, if you ever 'do less' (including leaving the room) and they are OK or less upset than they were when you were there, then stay away. Only go back if they are more upset.

At the opposite end of the scale, if your baby is always asleep at this stage after a couple of minutes of the technique, start putting them down a little earlier as you want them to be able to go to sleep even when they aren't 'completely ready' and pass out immediately. This is good and important practice for them.

HOW TO NOT ENCOURAGE THE PROTESTS, AND HOW TO REDUCE THE CRYING

When sleep training, parents often do things to try and reduce the crying that have the opposite effect. The things that they are doing are the very things that encourage the protests they are experiencing. This is especially the case when you spend too long on one stage.

The most common example is forgetting to 'do less' if baby protests. I completely understand why. If your baby is screaming all you want to do is stop them screaming, so what do you do? You naturally do more. You go back a stage, pat a little faster, give them a quick cuddle, or hold your hand on for longer 'until they settle'. All these things are 'doing more' and may give immediate respite from the crying but your baby will soon learn to cry to get you to do more.

Forgetting to do less is the biggest culprit of babies crying more and for a protest to escalate. Keep this in mind when making the changes and it'll be a much smoother process.

Doing more can be something subtle. Perhaps baby starts rolling and you roll them back without taking your hands away first, or baby starts standing and you lie them down before moving away first. Both of these will encourage that behaviour. However, if you 'do less' (and move away) first, and then lie them down or roll them over, they won't keep doing it. When your immediate reaction is to do less, you so won't encourage the behaviour.

GENTLE REMINDER OF THE KEY PRINCIPLES

At each stage of sleep training your baby will have a slightly new way of getting to sleep to get used to.

Babies love consistency so it's very normal for them to protest at each stage. It is difficult to predict which stages babies will take to well and which stages they will find more difficult. Some babies breeze through cot settling yet find it really difficult when you remove your hand.

Throughout the process, remember the key principles. If you remain calm, confident, and consistent, your baby will adapt to the changes. Baby will mimic your feelings so if you find the process hard, they will too. If you can be confident, consistent and calm with the changes, you will have a much better chance of your baby finding the process easier too. If you find you are a bit stuck, take a breath and consider how you feel about the changes.

If you lack confidence and are not being consistent, your baby will not adapt well to the changes. Take a deep breath, put relaxing music on some headphones, do some meditation, have a glass of wine – whatever you know will relax you, and go into bed time determined that it will work. Then it will. I have many phone calls from parents I'm working one-to-one with and things are going completely wrong. After one pep talk, they go away feeling determined to create change. Later I get a phone call saying everything is on track again.

MOVING FORWARD TO MODULE FIVE

As you approach the final stages of the course, module five is all about the finishing touches – ensuring you've tackled any remaining issues.

You may still have some issues with early mornings or nap lengths, but you will tackle those in the next two modules.

CHECKLIST: are you ready for module five?

Before moving to the next module *(Finishing Touches)* are the following true?

- Your baby's milk feeds are separate from all nap times and bed time.
- You are walking out of the room for bed/nap times and baby is going to sleep by themselves (more on this in module five so do read on even if you are a little stuck in the room).
- You are down to one overnight feed between bed time and morning.

At other wakes overnight, you are checking baby is ok and walking out.

MODULE FIVE: FINISHING TOUCHES

By this point your baby's sleep should have improved considerably but there may be some unresolved issues. These can make you feel like you haven't made progress. Keep a twenty-four-hour diary and compare it to the one you kept at the start of the programme. Put this below:

Also (without looking at your previous questionnaire), answer these questions again:

Score each statement in the following way…

- **Not an issue at all = 1 point**
- **Occasionally an issue = 2 points**
- **More of an issue than not = 3 points**
- **This is my baby = 4 points**

1. My baby relies on me to help them go to sleep at every nap and bed time. [___]
2. My baby will only contact nap. [___]
3. My baby wakes every time I try to transfer them. [___]
4. Bed times are a struggle and I end up in their room for over an hour. [___]
5. My baby's day is unpredictable. I never know what to expect. [___]

6. I feel anxious that my baby doesn't get enough sleep. [___]
7. My baby is fussy with their food and is not weaning onto solids. (Score one point if baby isn't weaning yet.) [___]
8. I am up multiple times in the night helping my baby get back to sleep. [___]
9. No one else can help me settle my baby. It's all down to me. [___]
10. I don't feel like I can cope with my baby's sleep any more. [___]
11. We have false starts or short naps every day. [___]

Put your answer here (total score): [___]

Compare your current diary and score with the ones you recorded at the beginning of this book. I hope you can see the improvement. The great thing about the human body is that we are good at adapting and forgetting how bad things were. This is how we cope. It can also mean we don't realise how much things improve in a process. Look back to see how far you have already come.

Now it's time to tackle those finishing touches so that you can enjoy the full benefits of your baby sleeping well.

EARLY MORNING WAKES AND STRETCHING SHORT NAPS

When you start sleep training, your initial focus must be on your baby achieving the skill of self-settling to sleep from being fully awake. Your baby has to learn a whole new skill to go from asleep to awake and back to sleep.

If your baby struggles with early morning wakes and cannot stretch their naps, the chances are they haven't yet mastered this skill and will need to practise more and have a little encouragement.

This will not be possible *until* they have cemented the awake-to-asleep skill. To clarify, this means you are able to put your baby into their cot and walk straight out of the room, with no hanging around and no sitting out of sight. This must have become normal and you rarely need to go back. If you haven't yet reached this point, focus on that first.

Once you have mastered the self-settling from awake for a minimum of a week, the early mornings and stretching of naps often follow naturally. These two skills are usually the final things to fall into place. It often happens a week to two weeks after self-settling has become completely normal for them and for you.

If these skills don't follow, here are some things you can do to encourage your baby:

RESETTLING DURING NAPS

If your baby wakes prematurely, less than forty-five minutes into their nap, try leaving them to see if they resettle. In the initial stages of resettling, babies tend to wake up for a bit, whinge, play or cry and then go back to sleep. A resettle isn't usually seamless at first. It's not unusual for babies to have some awake time between two naps, as opposed to one continuous sleep.

As your baby gets better at resettling, the awake gap in the middle should reduce and then you won't even notice it (unless you are watching on a video monitor – more on this to come). Try keeping music or white noise on continuously if your baby relies on this to go to sleep, not just for the initial settling period. You can also try popping in just before they usually wake to ensure all their sleep triggers are in place – their dummy, music, white noise, comforter, and so on.

If none of the above works you can 'sleep train'. Go in and help them settle by placing your hand on them and then leaving again. Then you reduce what you are doing.

This is more likely to work if baby wakes grumpy and tired. If they are happy and smiling when you go in, there is much less chance of them settling. Some babies are perfectly happy on shorter naps, and this is more often the case if your baby sleeps more than ten hours overnight.

RESETTLING EARLY MORNING

As your baby's night time approaches the morning they will become more and more aware of their surroundings and will dip in and out of light and deep sleep. Their sleep cycles might only be five or ten minutes long.

Their ability to resettle at this time comes down to practice: the more they practise the easier they will find it. Even if they resettle twice for five mins each time, that is excellent practice as they don't know how long they have been asleep for. Keep practising.

RESETTLING TIPS

If your baby has been relying on a small feed leading up to morning, you could try a stage that's slightly back from where you are in the day time (e.g. patting in the cot) and then move forward once they settle without the milk. It's fine if you need to be on a mattress in your baby's room for these early morning wakes, especially if they wake frequently, to prevent you needing to go in and out a lot. Focus on getting them settling back into their cot. If you use music or white noise, leaving it on at this time can also help with the resettling; also ensure your baby has their dummy if they use one.

If you are still offering one night-time feed, getting this as close as possible to the morning will help with the early mornings. Keep making the night feed later and later.

Pick your battles! If it gets to nine and a half hours after bed time and you've already resettled twice, it might be time to start the day. Practice makes perfect. Keep practising the wakes, try to do as little as possible, and reduce what you do just as you have during the rest of the twenty-four hours.

Note: early mornings and shorter naps go hand in hand with illness or teething. Be aware of this at these times.

DITCH THE VIDEO MONITOR

Get rid of your video monitor. This advice has worked time and time again for anxious, sleep-deprived parents. Many are surprised by this but it isn't until they do so that they get a good night's sleep.

This is why:

- **The parent *always* knows when baby is awake.** You may think this is a good thing, but it actually isn't. It is perfectly normal for a baby to wake from their sleep and drift off again after a while. You do not need to know every time your baby wakes.
- **A monitor makes it much harder for you to switch off** and not need to see your baby all the time.
- **If the video monitor goes upstairs with you when you go to bed**, it creates further problems. Your baby stirring may cause you to lie awake,

anxiously waiting for their next move. You wake each time your baby does, which you no longer need to.

- **It is like having an amplifier into your bedroom from your baby's room**. It is louder than having them in the room with you!

Unless you live in a very large house, or your baby is on another floor, there is no need to have even a sound monitor on overnight. If you must have one on, as you wouldn't hear them without, plug it in on the landing outside your room and turn the volume right down.

My job is predominantly to help parents relax and feel more confident. If there is one device that gets in the way of achieving this, it is the video monitor.

WALKING OUT THE ROOM – WHY THIS IS *NOT* CONTROLLED CRYING

I want to establish what we mean by 'walking out'.

For a lot of parents, the 'walking out of the room' stage initially feels like 'controlled crying' or 'cry it out'. While I understand where the comparisons come from, I assure you this final walking out of the room stage is nothing like CC or CIO.

All the training so far has prepared your baby for this final step. You have implemented routine changes, introduced sleep triggers, gradually removed you from their sleep routine, and have ensured they can self-settle. This final step of walking out is just another very small, manageable step.

A lot of parents get very comfortable when they reach the stage of standing in the room and many are tempted to stay at that stage. I strongly advise you not to. You are so close to finishing, but you've not yet got to the end of the sleep tightrope. If there is any regression due to teething or illness, you will likely take significant backward steps, and inevitably fall off. Once your baby can completely self-settle without you in the room, there is far less risk of regressions. *Do not stop just before you get to the finish line.*

Cross that finish line and then you'll be ready for these final, finishing touches. This is the stage you've been preparing your baby for all long. Controlled crying would have been doing this right at the beginning of the book. In fact, it would have been putting your baby into their cot and walking out without even reading this book.

ELIMINATING THE FINAL NIGHT-TIME FEED

Once you complete the training process it is important to eliminate that final night feed. This can be done in two ways.

If you are breastfeeding you can slowly move this feed forward. Put in a curfew of after two am, then after three am, and after four am, and so on, until they have eliminated that feed. You can also reduce the time on the breast by keeping it steady at ten minutes for three days and then nine minutes for three days until you've eliminated it completely.

If you are combination or bottle-feeding, this process is even easier. Move the feed forward as per the above instructions until you get it to after two am. Once you achieve this, swap the breast feed to a bottle and then slowly reduce the quantity of milk in the bottle. If your baby is taking six ounces, reduce this to five and then four and so on, until you've eliminated the milk.

At first, when you start to reduce the amount of milk in the bottle or the amount of time on the breast, your baby might cry when you take them off. Do not put them back on the breast or offer more milk, because this will encourage protests. Hold them and cuddle until they are calm, then put them back into the cot before they go to sleep, to self-settle in there as they do at other times.

When you shorten the feed, if your baby starts waking earlier in the morning this may be an indication of hunger. If this happens, I advise putting the reduction in the night-time feed on hold at whatever time or quantity you have reached. Wait for baby to catch up with the reduction in calories in the day time. You will know when they have done this as they will no longer wake earlier and hungry in the morning. Then start reducing again. Some babies need a night-time feed until they are ten months.

MODULE SIX: MOVING FORWARD WITH YOUR BABY SLEEPING WELL

The advice in this section is offered from one mummy to another. I am a qualified nurse, and I have nursed many a sick baby, but this is not intended as a replacement for medical advice. Always seek help from your GP, paediatrician, pharmacist or medical centre if you are worried about your baby.

SLEEP REGRESSIONS

Sleep regressions happen for many reasons. The most noted ones happen around developmental leaps such as the four-month sleep regression I talked about in the introduction. Each time your baby learns something new, their sleep needs reduce. They are learning and need more time for that learning. This can trigger a 'sleep regression'. Baby can wake in the night and practise their new skill of sitting up, for example. Or they need later bed or nap times. If your little one starts protesting when going to sleep, increase those awake windows (also see the information in module three about nap transitions).

There will be regressions linked to travelling, teething, illness and pain (all covered in this chapter) but the most important thing is, if your baby already self-settles to sleep the regressions will be temporary. You will also be able to apply the principles to get back on track – just like Victoria did:

> *I've been following Hannah's programme since my twins were around four weeks old. I'd competed the programme and had perfectly self-settling babies who were feeding and sleeping very well.*
>
> *When one twin became unwell at eight months old, firstly with a cold and then a sickness bug, I took the easy route and started taking her out the cot and rocking to sleep to avoid waking her sister.*
>
> *I went from having two babies who slept pretty much perfectly to one who needed constant contact to sleep, while the other continued to sleep independently.*
>
> *It was tiresome and the broken nights were making it so difficult to function. I was so worried I'd undone almost eight months of work. So, we went back to basics with the programme. I revisited the course and, with a little help from Hannah, had a perfectly settled baby back in her own cot after three nights.*

I have every confidence that when sickness strikes again we can get back on track quickly so everyone can have a good night's sleep and wake up happy!

You really have been a god send to us, Hannah,

— *VIC.*

This highlights just how important it is to get to self-settling, as the regressions will then be temporary.

ILLNESS AND TEETHING, AND HOW THEY IMPACT SLEEP

It is normal for babies and toddlers to have many infections in the first few years of life. In fact, this is an important way of ensuring their immune systems are primed to fight disease and infection.

It is not unusual for babies to get up to fifteen colds in their first two years, each time building their immune system and teaching it how to react to illness. Did you know you only ever get the same cold once? Each virus you get is a new one, which is why adults often don't get poorly when children do. We have that immunity already.

Babies often have a more extreme reaction to infection too, spiking temperatures when we wouldn't. Again, this is normal. Babies' immune systems are immature, and a temperature is another way of killing off the bacteria or virus causing the illness.

Unfortunately, especially if your baby or toddler is in child-care, illnesses are hard to avoid, and so are the sleepless nights that go hand-in-hand. If they are lucky enough to avoid the bugs in the first few years, they will certainly suffer when they start school.

So how can we avoid illness, what can you do to help your baby if they are poorly, and how do you get back on track once they are better?

SOME TIPS FOR AVOIDING ILLNESS

First things first; hand washing. I can't over-emphasise how important this is. Washing hands is vital every time they have anything to eat and when returning home. We have all become used to using hand sanitiser when out and about too – if the pandemic has taught us one thing, it is the importance of hand sanitising to help stop the spread of infection.

Another thing that greatly helps prevent the spread of infection from outside the home to inside is removing shoes in the house. This is especially important when you have a crawler but ideally do this with children of all ages. Germs from your shoes are spread when worn in the home. Also ensure the places you visit are clean. The biggest culprits are soft play centres – they are excellent fun, but choose wisely and ideally go at the beginning of the day. Fresh air is great for the immune system; the more air, the fewer bugs. Take walks, meet outside and keep windows open in the house when possible.

Also consider your baby's diet. A good diet with different colourful fruits and vegetables boosts the immune system. Tropical fruit is great for vitamin and mineral levels, as are berries, peppers and green leafy vegetables. Variety is the key.

Another dietary culprit that puts a strain on the immune system is sugar. The body has to use up many vitamins and minerals when processing it, and in order to maintain blood sugar levels. Be careful of hidden sugars in yoghurts, cereals, cereal bars, fruit juice, snacks such fruit bars, and even raisins. Ideally the only sugar your baby/toddler consumes daily should be that from whole fruit.

I also advise supplementing key vitamins if you worry that your baby or toddler doesn't take enough through their diet or they could do with a boost. A good liquid multi vitamin is great for your baby. Vitamin D is advised for all babies and toddlers, especially in the winter months. I advise probiotics: I think they are a great addition to any baby's diet. This is especially the case if they (or you if breast feeding) have ever needed antibiotics, suffered from thrush, or you had a c-section birth as your baby hasn't had the population of bacteria from the birthing canal.

HELPING YOUR POORLY BABY, AND MINIMISING SLEEP REGRESSIONS

The first few times your baby is poorly are heart breaking. Every parent wishes they could take the illness away and have it themselves. Babies go downhill very quickly but also tend to bounce back very quickly.

Alongside illness usually comes sleep regression. Even the best of sleepers who are in a good routine and sleeping independently before illness hits often revert to screaming at nap time, needing lots of cuddles and being awake for much of the night. This is even more apparent in babies who are poor sleepers. So how can you help your baby?

COLDS/COUGHS AND BRONCHIOLITIS

A baby's cough or cold can have an immediate impact on sleep. They find it hard to be flat so in an *older toddler* a pillow can help. A reflux wedge can be an easy and safe way to raise your baby slightly to help them. Some babies also find relief from steaming (take baby into a bathroom with the shower on and sit on the toilet) especially before bed or at nap times.

There are some great products on the market to help. As babies can't blow their noses one of the most useful is a nasal sucker. This is especially helpful to clear snot just before feeding. Saline drops or sprays can work brilliantly alongside sucking to make the snot easier to remove. Vapour rubs or essential oils also offer relief, especially overnight.

I am a great advocate of natural essential oils to help your family. There are many essential oils that support the immune system and are safe and natural even on the smallest of babies. Although extremely safe it is important to choose wisely and to know what you are using and how to use them – especially with little ones. I have many resources on issues like this in my community.

Babies often get a temperature with even the slightest cold. This is perfectly normal in young babies especially, due to their immature immune system. Similarly, it is normal for babies with a slight cold to go off their milk and solid feeds. A full tummy makes it even harder for them to breathe easily so offer small feeds more often until they are better.

Colds are an 'upper respiratory tract infection' and are very common in babies. Occasionally, mainly due to the small distance between your baby's nose and chest, this can become more serious and become a lower respiratory tract infection. Bronchiolitis is one example of this and babies can go downhill very quickly. Bronchiolitis can be viral or bacterial (RSV positive). If it is bacterial, babies might need antibiotics and sometimes hospital treatment.

If your baby shows signs of respiratory distress you must get medical help quickly. This can be seen in their nostrils flaring, sucking in in-between their ribs, or below their ribs (look up videos of intercostal recession or sub-costal recession) or tracheal tug. If your baby has any of these symptoms, I would want them seen within an hour… or call emergency services.

CROUP

Croup is characterised by a barking 'seal-like' cough. It sounds terrible and is often confused with choking in a baby. It is not unusual for parents to call an ambulance the first time they hear it. Surprisingly, just having the cough is not at all dangerous; you just need to watch for any breathing difficulties. Croup is a virus so there is no treatment; the only time clinicians intervene is if baby is struggling to breathe. At this point steroids can be prescribed.

Taking a baby into fresh, cold air often helps as it reduces inflammation in the airway and often stops the coughing, as does steaming. Croup is often worse at night so opening a window and standing next to it is a good first step if baby is struggling. If you are worried, please do seek emergency help. Never try to drive a baby to A&E on your own if they have breathing difficulties. Babies can go downhill quickly so call emergency services.

DIARRHOEA AND VOMITING

This spreads so quickly; one member of the family catches it and the whole family becomes ill. Unfortunately, there is little medically that can be done to stop the symptoms. It is a case of riding it out.

The main risk in children is dehydration so encouraging fluids is essential: plenty of water, watered down coconut water, breast milk or formula. If baby is weaned and it is a severe bug, I find stopping all solids for twelve hours to allow the tummy to rest can help. Babies and small children often eat in-between bouts of sickness and this can lengthen the illness. If your baby shows signs of dehydration (fewer wet nappies, lethargy, sunken in the soft spot on their head), seek medical help.

If severely dehydrated your GP health professional may advise rehydration salts so it may be worth keeping some in your medicine cabinet just in case. Coconut water is also great for hydrating even the youngest of weaned babies.

You are infectious for forty-eight hours after all symptoms have ended so avoid coming into contact with anyone during this time. Even a mild tummy bug in you or your toddler could be much more serious in the elderly or a small baby.

TEMPERATURE CONTROL

If your under-four-year-old has a temperature it is important not to do anything that may increase it further. Keep the room temperature on the lower side, dress them in cool, loose clothing and ideally don't cuddle to sleep. If they won't sleep in their cot, try them lying next to you.

Remember the temperature is there for a reason. It is very useful in fighting viruses and bacteria, both of which are highly sensitive to a change in temperature. Babies have an immature immune system and one of their main tools for fighting off infection is raising body temperature. Because of this, NHS advice is to give paracetamol or ibuprofen only if your baby is miserable with a temperature, so that you can ensure that your baby is comfortable, but also give the temperature a chance to do its job. Often parents take a temperature as a reason in itself to offer medication. If you bring the temperature down unnecessarily, it is not able to do its job of fighting the illness.

The other important matter with a baby with a temperature is knowing why they have it: the source of the infection. If they have cold symptoms, or a cough, or are vomiting, then you know why they have a temperature. If they are asymptomatic (have no symptoms), you really need to find out why they have a temperature. It could be that your little one has a urine infection, or an ear infection. A temperature without obvious symptoms is definitely a reason to seek medical advice.

But, if your baby is miserable and clingy, which often indicates they are in pain, giving paracetamol or ibuprofen will help with the pain so can be offered for that reason.

FEBRILE CONVULSIONS

A febrile convulsion is a convulsion in a baby or child which is only associated with the temperature. It has no links to epilepsy. Your baby will only suffer from these convulsions when they have a high temperature; this is how this type of convulsion is characterised and diagnosed. Although rare, and frightening, I would like to reassure you that if your baby does suffer from them, they have no lasting effects and baby will grow out of them.

They happen because babies don't have any way of managing their own temperature; the hypothalamus is not mature enough to bring the temperature down itself. If your baby overheats this is a way of 'fanning' their body to reduce the temperature.

The best thing you can do is make sure your baby is safe, and that they can't hurt themselves, maybe on a carpeted floor. Stay calm and call an ambulance. You may be advised to give your baby Calpol or Nurofen once they come round to bring down the temperature and avoid another seizure. These episodes are almost unheard of in children over the age of five, once the hypothalamus kicks in.

PAIN SYMPTOMS AND MANAGEMENT

Remember that pain usually goes hand-in-hand with a cold, cough or tummy bug. If your baby is miserable you must try to ensure they're pain free. Usually the only symptoms of pain in a baby are being clingy, miserable, not wanting to be put down, frequent wakes and shorter naps. Even if they don't have a temperature, they could still be uncomfortable. Think about when you have a cold. Often the outward symptom of a cold is 'just a snotty nose' but inside you might feel really poorly, have a terrible headache and sore throat. It is the same for your baby. If your baby has slight symptoms, and is grumpy, clingy, hard to manage and their sleep has regressed, please ensure they are pain free.

TEETHING

Unlike most illnesses teething can go on for weeks, sometimes months. Babies who are self-settling are often less disturbed by teething, simply because if something is just bothering them a little they are able to sleep through it. If your baby isn't self-settling, focus on that first to ensure that they are able to be less disturbed by any teething episode. Keep working through the programme unless the teething is in an acute stage.

If your baby is acutely teething, the top priority is to keep pain-free. For this, you have a few options. If the tooth is just popping through you may want to consider baby paracetamol or ibuprofen; these are obviously medicine-based painkillers and you need to ensure that you follow the instructions on the side of the bottle and consult your pharmacist if you have any questions.

If you would like to use more natural remedies, you could use essential oils. Clove oil or lavender oil are great for teething, as are ylang ylang and frankincense.

You can also get topical creams, gels or liquids to go onto the gum, or powders.

It's worth experimenting as what suits one baby doesn't necessarily suit another, and you may need different remedies at different times – teeth moving around in the gums is a very different sensation from a tooth breaking through.

In the day time you can help the process by letting your baby chew down on things like teething rings that you keep in the fridge or cold pieces of fruit or vegetables. The more your baby bites down the quicker the teeth will come through and the quicker it'll pass.

GETTING BACK ON TRACK WITH SLEEP (AND MINIMISING REGRESSIONS WHEN POORLY)

Unfortunately, it's virtually impossible to avoid sleep regressions with a poorly baby, but if your baby was sleeping independently before the illness, they will remember the skill; they may just need reminding once they're feeling better that they can do it.

First things first, when they are poorly, don't panic. The first few times your baby is poorly, it will seem like everything is going wrong and it will never be resolved.

I receive lots of calls from panicked parents whose good sleeper is poorly and is now up fifteen times a night. I always ask them to get back in touch about sleep once the symptoms have subsided and they are eating normally again. When I speak to them ten days later, the majority have fallen back into their old routine of good sleep. Those who haven't tend to do so after a little advice and a couple more days.

There are things you can do whilst they're poorly that will make things as easy as possible for you all to get back to good sleep when they're feeling better.

Firstly, try to practise putting them into their cot awake and settling by themselves at least once in twenty-four hours. Try as much as possible to stick to their usual bedtime routine and incorporate the sleep triggers you use, even if they need to sleep next to you in the midst of illness.

If you can, keep them in their own bed. You can camp on their floor if you need to keep an eye on them. It is ideal for them to remain in their usual sleeping place. This is also usually the safest place for them to be.

Once the main symptoms have eased, they seem less clingy and are eating well, that's usually a good indication that they are 'better'. This could be a few days after the acute symptoms such as temperature have subsided. At this point, get back on track as soon as possible.

The starting point is to get back into your old routine with meal and feed times, sleep and bed times. Once the routine is back in place, concentrate on your baby or toddler going to sleep independently. This will be a short process if they were doing this before becoming poorly.

It will be more of a challenge for babies who have never learned this skill. If you have yet to reach the end of the sleep training, work out what stage you had reached from the table in module four. Most importantly, stick to 'doing less' if baby protests. Stick to that stage for a few days while your baby recovers fully before moving forward and continuing with the process.

Your baby *will* get back on track. Here are a few reassuring words from people in the same position as you:

> *We had finished Hannah's programme and things were good: everyone was sleeping. We then hit teething, croup and tonsillitis back to back and sleep went totally downhill. I could feel all my old anxieties creeping back in with the sleepless nights but we went back a step on the programme for a few nights and once she was better, everything went back to normal and I realised that we could always get back on track quite quickly by referring back to the course and being consistent.*
>
> — *HAYLEY*

TIPS TO HELP YOU IN A SLEEP CRISIS

No matter how good a sleeper you have, there will be times your baby can't sleep.

There may be reasons for this – illness, teething or vaccinations are the most common ones. Other times there won't. It's virtually impossible to avoid a sleep crisis at some point when you have a baby.

So – what do you do when that sleep crisis hits? First things first, stop documenting, turn off that app, put your pen and paper down. If your baby is going through a sleep crisis, documenting every minute or hour they're awake will just make you more anxious. Keep your phone away from your bed if you can. Looking at the time or popping onto Facebook will mean even less time resting or sleeping. When you have a window to sleep, sleep.

Interestingly, research has shown that a twenty-minute nap can undo the hormonal imbalance from a whole night's bad sleep. If you can grab a nap then do, no matter how short. Sometimes the little power naps are the most restorative. It is also fine to co-sleep for some of the night, as long as it is safe to do so (look up the lullaby guidelines on this). If your baby is really unsettled this can mean you get better sleep. If your baby was sleeping independently before the sleep crisis, they will remember how to do this again. Just make sure to practise sleeping independently each day, maybe for a nap or bedtime settle, but you don't need to fight to keep your baby in the cot the whole twenty-four hours.

Please also remember to ask for help. We mummies are so bad at this. Call in a friend to take baby for a walk, pass baby to your partner and go and sleep for the evening, or ask your parents to watch baby for an hour or two so you can have a bath and a sleep. Get some fresh air. I know it's the last thing you feel like doing but getting out for a walk not only helps you, it will also help baby.

Although it is tempting to let baby sleep when they are managing to, try to avoid baby compensating too much by sleeping lots in the day as this can lead to another bad night. If they do nap, ensure you rest too. Even if you can't sleep, put your feet up and ignore the housework – it can wait. You don't need to be superwoman. The laundry, dishes and hoovering can wait for a less exhausted person or time.

It is also good to share the load. If baby is up all night, take shifts. You could go to bed at seven pm with your partner doing seven pm to one am, then you take over. Or you could do the first part and your partner then takes over to let you sleep in the morning. If your partner is working and you can't share, try to get even a few hours of baby free sleep time. This can be managed by you going to bed early, or your partner getting up early. For example, if you take the night shift, they get up with baby at five am and have them for two or three hours before they head off to work.

Don't neglect yourself. Remember the 'oxygen mask' rule on an aeroplane – you must look after yourself first to be able to help your child. I know this is hard but take some time out, even if it is five minutes.

Look after yourself, keep hydrated and don't forget to eat. If you aren't eating as well as not sleeping you'll feel much worse. Aim for protein and fat-based foods – nuts, hummus, meat, fish, cheese, avocado. These release slow energy for you to tap into. Being dehydrated can cause lethargy so keep up with water too.

Finally, you are only human. It is normal to feel angry, cross, upset, frustrated, or all of these. Put baby somewhere safe, walk away, take some deep breaths, call a friend, ask for help. Every single parent has felt like this. You are not a bad parent for being human.

REFLUX AND COW'S MILK PROTEIN ALLERGY

Cow's milk protein (CMP) is part of cow's milk. It is often mistaken for lactose which is a different part of the milk. CMP is the protein element and lactose is the sugar element. Babies and children react to the protein in milk far more commonly than the lactose.

Milk allergy can be either immunoglobulin E (IgE) or non-IgE mediated. IgE-mediated reactions typically occur immediately after ingestion whereas non-IgE mediated are delayed and take up to forty-eight hours to develop. Both involve the immune system.

IgE CMP allergy is rare, affecting between three and six percent of infants. Babies are usually diagnosed pretty early on as symptoms can be immediate and severe – hives, breathing difficulties.

Non-IgE CMPA (what was always described as intolerance) is more common. It has less immediate symptoms but can still be severe – tummy cramps, blood in the stool, eczema, other skin reactions, colic, wind and reflux, and sleep issues. All of these can lead to an unsettled baby.

I've certainly found – with my own children and others – that reflux symptoms can disappear when an intolerance to cow's milk protein is addressed, and studies have found this to be true. Therefore, I regularly advise trialling a CMP-free diet for babies that come to me with reflux symptoms.

This is particularly my recommendation for a baby who has two or more of the following:

- A history of colic
- Possible or firm diagnosis of reflux
- Eczema
- Ear infections
- More than two courses of antibiotics
- Mucus or blood in the stool
- Constipation or diarrhoea

Exclusion means removing all milk products from the diet – also from Mum's diet if breastfeeding. This includes all butter, cheese, yogurt and products that contain milk too.

Many mums find it useful to also trial a more thorough exclusion diet when breastfeeding, to assess further possible intolerances or aggravation to baby's tummy. All of the foods I advise excluding are in the breast-feeding exclusion diet below.

If you are formula feeding, the first thing I advise is trialling goat's milk formula. The protein molecules in goat's milk are different to those in cow's milk formula and the majority of babies that are non-IgE CMPA can tolerate goat's milk. If this doesn't suit your baby, contact your GP or paediatrician to get a prescription formula.

REFLUX TIPS

Reflux is far more common in babies than adults because babies spend more time on their back, their tummy is closer to their mouth, they have undeveloped muscles at the top of their stomach and have a predominantly liquid diet.

If baby seems to be unsettled and in pain after feeds, is back arching, can't be laid down for nappy changes or sleep, and is generally unsettled, reflux is a possibility. If the symptoms are severe, mention this to your GP or paediatrician.

Luckily, the changes you make with the programme will help your baby's reflux. Separating feeding and sleep is vital when babies have reflux as you want your baby to be able to lie down to sleep and this is impossible if they have a tummy full of milk. Similarly, reducing night-time feeds and separating your baby's bedtime feed and going to bed will also help.

Babies that wean well and increase solids also tend to grow out of their reflux as solid foods are more likely to stay in the tummy. Follow the weaning steps to get baby eating well.

The only thing more difficult for a parent of a reflux baby when sleep training is hearing baby cry. If you know your little one has been uncomfortable in the past and you've battled with extensive crying, it might be hard to listen to your baby cry when you make the changes. If your little one was fine before you started the technique and then starts crying and back arching immediately, this is almost certainly because of a protest rather than pain. Be calm, consistent and confident and your baby will adapt.

CMPA and reflux babies have in common more generally disturbed sleep. It is like having a baby with a constant mild cold or teething symptoms. They are always a little bit uncomfortable, and this can lead to their sleep being more disturbed.

In module one I talked about babies' short sleep cycles and their need to wake up. If your baby is slightly uncomfortable this can cause them to wake up more from these natural sleep cycles.

Once your baby is sleeping well then, even if they do wake more, they will be able to get themselves back off again. This is the beauty of the training. For this reason, I think sleep training babies with reflux, CMPA and other medial issues is even more important than training a baby without these symptoms.

Giving your baby a more predictable day, removing feeding to sleep, separating feeding and sleep, letting their tummy rest overnight, feeding them the right foods, and teaching them the skill of settling independently will also help with their symptoms. Lots of babies' reflux symptoms improve significantly with the steps we take in the programme. A number have even managed to come off their medication – of course, only do this under the advice of your doctor.

EXCLUSION DIET FOR BREASTFEEDING

Sometimes it is appropriate to investigate if the foods Mum is eating are affecting the baby through the breast milk. For this I advise a full exclusion diet, just for a few days, to see if there is any change in baby's symptoms. It will only take a few days to work out, and then you can reintroduce the foods (all at once if it hasn't made any difference or one by one if it has).

Below is a list of foods to avoid, some suggestions for alternatives and some excellent foods to include in your diet. You need to keep your calories up!

Foods to avoid:

All dairy (milk, yoghurt, butter, ice cream, cheese, chocolate, some crackers, some biscuits with butter, cottage cheese, cream cheese, cream, etc.)

In a week or so, experiment with goat's and sheep's milk products but keep those and all lactose free products eliminated for now.

Dairy alternatives: *almond or coconut milk, coconut oil, olive oil, olive spread (avoid other margarines), coconut yoghurt, coconut milk or cream (great in a smoothie).*

All wheat: bread, pasta, biscuits, crackers, some oatcakes, cake, couscous, bulgar wheat, some crisps.

Wheat alternatives: *popcorn, rice cakes and crackers, corn thins and corn crispbreads, gluten-free bread and gluten-free pasta, rice, quinoa, pearl barley, lentils, sweet potato, potatoes, potato crisps, nuts and seeds.*

Other foods to be eliminated: strawberries, tomatoes, kiwi fruit, chilli, caffeine, onion, peppers, garlic.

Keep the following to a minimum: eggs, white potato.

Excellent foods to include in your diet:

Avocado, coconut oil, coconut milk, coconut yogurt, all meat (apart from beef), all fish, nuts, seeds, all vegetables and fruits (apart from listed), sweet potatoes, salad, dahl, rice.

Keep your calories up and drink plenty of water too.

You will see the difference in your baby within a week of making these changes if one of these foods is the cause of the problem. If there is no difference, go back to your old diet. If it does make a difference, keep to the full exclusion diet for two weeks and then reintroduce foods one at a time, no more than one every four days. If the symptoms return, eliminate that food again. If the new food makes no difference, that food is ok to eat.

TIPS FOR TRAVELLING, MANAGING HOLIDAYS, GOING OUT, AND NAPS ON THE GO

I don't want you to put life on hold while you complete that process. Yes, you need to practise regularly and have a set-up (cot, mattress, sleep triggers) in place for the practice but I want you to continue with normal life. If this means weekends in the country, meals out, visiting relatives or a week's camping trip in the middle of the programme, go for it. Help your baby learn to sleep well while participating in what normal life means to you. If you put your whole life on hold for a sleep programme, the chances are it'll unravel when you start to enjoy the things you want to enjoy as a family.

When completing the training, if you are in new surroundings take with you as many familiar things as you can. Take a sheet from home, your baby's music or white noise, stick to the same sleep triggers and they should adapt well.

Once you get to cot settling, it is vital you stick to baby sleeping in a cot. If you co-sleep for convenience each time you go away, it'll be much harder to get back on track once home.

You can also practise sleeping in the travel cot at home, in their usual room. This can ease the transition while away. Ensure the travel cot has a comfortable mattress and if your family likes to visit places overnight, I would invest in your own travel cot so your baby becomes familiar with it, despite most hotels offering to provide one.

If your baby finds it hard to settle the first nap or bed time when you are away, staying in the room and pottering around is best, even if you are at the walking out stage. If you aren't quite there yet, going one step back in the table in module four while they adjust to the new surroundings is also fine.

While away it is important to practise settling. This is especially the case if you travel frequently or for long periods. If you don't practise the settling for a minimum of one nap and/or bed time each day, you'll find it hard to get back on track each time.

If you are in a hotel room, you can achieve this putting baby down in the cot and going into the bathroom or onto the balcony for nap time or bed time. It is even ok to practise this at bed time and then take baby out for the evening. Just go through their usual bedtime routine, put them into the cot, go into the bathroom and get yourself ready. Lift baby out of the cot once they have self-settled and put them into the pram to go out for the evening.

If your baby wakes overnight and you are unable to settle them, maybe because you are aware of waking others in the house or hotel, don't worry too much if things go back a little. The important thing is to get back on track as soon as you are home. As long as you have practised the settling this shouldn't be too hard – a couple of nights and you'll be back on track.

OUT AND ABOUT NAPS

Some babies sleep brilliantly when out and about, and some find it much more difficult. Like anything sleep related, it's just practice. If you want your baby to be able to sleep in a stationary pram, for example, then practise. Start with naps at home where you don't mind if there is a little whinging. Have the TV or radio on in the background as it's rare you'll be somewhere silent for an out and about nap. Initially rock your baby a little in the pram but slowly reduce this. Practise for one nap a day and your baby will soon get used to this. This becomes easier as you go through the table in module four and get baby sleeping more independently. White noise or music can help, as can putting a muslin over the pram so they aren't distracted by external goings on.

MANIPULATING THE ROUTINE FOR SOCIAL EVENTS

You may also use extra or longer naps to make bed time later on purpose. You might want to do this on holiday, or if you are going out in the evening, or at a festival. Let them have a longer nap so they aren't tired until later in the evening. This means you can enjoy the evening out with them not being grumpy and tired.

SOME TIPS FOR WORKING PARENTS

As a working mummy myself, and one who went back to work each time before my baby was a month old, I know and appreciate the extra strain working alongside having a baby can bring. I also appreciate how vital it is for some people to have both baby and work. I would have found it incredibly hard to be a stay at home parent. I value the variety of working and having a family.

There are many kinds of working parents, and I know that no matter what kind you are this comes with mixed feelings and often a lot of guilt. If you go back to work early like me, but with baby alongside you, you will feel guilty about not giving one hundred percent to either. If you head back to the office after a long maternity but it means you aren't there for those school pick ups and maybe only get to see your little one for a few hours a day, it's hard.

I know from working with many families, over many years, that mummy guilt is real. I also know for a fact that every parent is doing the best for their family. Finally, I know that babies adapt. Whatever your working situation, this is 'normal' for your baby.

Here are some issues to consider when sleep training a baby while you are working. The first is practice. It is great if your childcare provider will mimic the sleep training and be on board with the steps. If you have a nanny, or a relative is providing childcare, this may well be possible. I do appreciate that some relatives might not be on board. If this is the case, it is fine for them to opt for pram or car naps. Just try to ensure they are not feeding to sleep, or trying the technique and doing something else when it fails.

What if your baby is in a nursery? Speak to them; some nurseries are happy to mimic your settling technique, so if you are patting in the cot they will too. If this isn't possible, let them do their thing and you focus on bed times and overnight.

What if you have bought this book because you are heading back to work after maternity leave? This is one of the main reasons parents contact me for sleep support. Work is looming and they know they can't function on the sleep they currently get. Many companies are looking into offering parental sleep support for this reason. Sleep isn't just a nice to have: it is vital. This is even more the case if you need to travel to or function in work. In some cases it means the difference between practising safely and not being safe to practise. I have a whole page dedicated to corporate support for working parents, if this is something your workplace might consider.

For you as an individual, the changes you make now will make your situation better in a week, even better in two, and you could be sleeping well in three to four weeks' time. If you don't have the luxury of four weeks before you go back to work, move through the stages more quickly. Some parents complete all the changes in two to three weeks.

If you would like more support, my sleep course will guide you through the changes, complete with video tutorials and worksheets to reinforce the information. This can all be found in your Sleep Well Hub via the QR code link on the inside cover.

SUMMARY CHAPTER: CONCLUSION TO THE SLEEP PROGRAMME

ABOUT MY ONLINE COURSE AND SUPPORT

I officially started helping babies sleep well in 2008. Between then and 2020 I mainly worked one-to-one with parents as well as delivering in-person talks for charities, the NHS and children's centres. Just as it did for many people, everything changed a short way into 2020 and I had to adapt how I worked. This wasn't because I had to transition to working from home. I had always worked this way, and rarely met any of the families I worked with. But I was suddenly so much in demand: so many families needed me and my support. NHS resources were pulled from postnatal care, drop-in clinics shut and new parents were struggling. I went from having three to five enquiries a week to hundreds. This led me to set up my online community which grew to 25,000 in less than three years, to focus on my social media, and to set up my online course – Sleep Well, with Hannah. This book is a continuation of this development, and with it I hope to help even more people. If you feel you would like more support on your Sleep Well journey, please reach out to me on Instagram or Facebook or join my community. I would love to support you and your baby to Sleep Well.

Here you can find my online course:

https://sleepwellwithhannah.com/sleep-solutions/

I hope you have found this book helpful and reassuring. Above all, I hope you manage to follow the steps to get your baby sleeping well. Baby sleep is an on-going process and there will be bumps in the road and regressions. At these times, refer back to the information and re-follow the steps to get baby sleeping well again.

I would love to hear how you are getting on. I absolutely love hearing the transformations that people have made. Please pop over to Amazon and Trustpilot and leave me a review, and let me know how you and your family are sleeping.

Here are my social links if you would like any further support on your parenting journey.

https://www.facebook.com/groups/yummybabysleepwell

www.instagram.com/sleep_well_with_hannah

You can also see all my parenting courses and support on my website:

www.sleepwellwithhannah.com

Finally, go back and re-visit your reasons for being here. Can you now manage them? I truly hope so. I hope this journey has been everything I promised.

Most importantly, I hope your whole family is sleeping well.

Hannah Love

KIND WORDS BY ANDREW

“*Our daughter is self-settling into her morning nap on a sunny day in May. We know she'll settle and during her naps we are getting free time! We're staying with grand-parents so no chores!*

The bleak, pre-Hannah, sleep-deprived, anxiety-ridden winter is behind us.

You brought us here. You carried us to sanity. Thank you.

The definition of insanity is doing the same thing and expecting different results. We were stuck in a trap that must affect so many parents – it's amazing there aren't more people like you out there. I hope you realise how good you are at what you do.

When my wife told me that she wanted to enlist your support to help our six-month-old I was sceptical as we'd just had a mostly negative experience with the previous sleep trainer. We had hoped that doing our daughter's first sleep training over the Christmas holidays (with the previous trainer) would be an ideal opportunity for us to work together and break all the bad habits that we'd fallen into. It wasn't a happy Christmas break as before long the small improvements were a distant memory and we'd reverted back to where we started.

When we got in touch with you (Hannah) our daughter would only nap in a sling and was waking up to eight times a night and required feeding back to sleep.

We were so desperate for help we were on our knees. Family life had become totally unmanageable: my wife was suffering physically and emotionally and we were totally reliant on her amazing parents for support.

For anyone reading this who thinks Hannah's success rate sounds too good to be true, you need to have faith. **It does work.** *Just follow the steps and have faith.*

After completing your training I am so glad that that my scepticism didn't prevent us from getting what we needed.

Hat's off to you Hannah – you gave us exactly what we needed, when we needed it and in such a supportive way. You have such wide knowledge covering far more than just sleep and you are especially skilled in remaining supportive.

It's a credit to you, my wife's persistence, and my amazing in laws that I can now spend time doing things that were beyond my wildest dreams a few months ago: having meals out with my wife, taking our daughter to restaurants, re-building my professional network and thinking about my future again.

I hope we meet one day and I get to hug you, for my gratitude is beyond words.

— *ANDREW.*

ABOUT THE AUTHOR

It was August bank holiday weekend. My waters had broken and I was being driven at midnight to the same hospital I was born in almost exactly thirty years earlier. Forty-eight hours later, after a transfer to another hospital for an emergency C-section, my first baby, Oliver, was born. All I ever wanted was to be a mummy and here I was holding my new baby boy. The love was overwhelming but so was the sense of fear, anxiety and 'what the f**k have I just been through'.

My whole life had led to this point. When I was a small child, my bedroom was a nursery for my dolly, Benjamin, and as soon as I was old enough I started babysitting. On leaving school I enrolled at King's College London to train as a Children's Nurse, graduating in 2000. As soon as I qualified I was contacted with an amazing nannying opportunity. I spent the early 2000s travelling around the world as a Nanny for professional sports personalities – trusted to travel independently with their children across the globe. It was my job to have them sleeping (and behaving) well. I helped run the households, juggling the children, washing, cleaning, cooking, admin tasks and generally organising the families I worked for while home and away.

I was then approached about a private nursing position for a family with nine children and a very poorly baby. Both parents were doctors and they needed a nurse to help with the baby, as well as the other children. I was in my element, nursing but also nannying at the same time. As my feet were more permanently in the UK, I decided to enrol in two university courses, one to become a Nutritional Therapist and another to become a Craniosacral Therapist. Three years later I graduated.

A job came up with an old golfing family who agreed for me to work three days a week, which left me time to work as the Principle Paediatric Nutritional Therapist for the National Nutrition Clinic, as well as take weaning and first aid classes from a company called Baby-Steps. I set up my nutrition business, Yummy Nutrition, and started helping families.

It was in these sessions that I started being asked about baby sleep. I always introduced myself and explained my background, and no matter what the consultation or training session was meant to be about, it always diverted to baby sleep. The parents were struggling and there was little or no sleep help. I remember googling 'sleep training baby' in 2008 and there was not one person offering that service. I knew what I had to do.

While pregnant with Oliver I changed my business name from Yummy Nutrition to 'Yummy Baby Group'. I offered nutritional consultations, supernanny consultations, weaning calls and sleep programmes. All anyone wanted to book was a sleep programme.

I built up my business alongside my job as Nanny which Oliver joined me at when he was just a few weeks old. By the time our second daughter Ella came along in 2012, my sleep training business was blooming and I had given up nannying. I was helping so many families that I had little to no maternity leave with Ella, or with Henry who arrived in 2015.

Parenthood taught me things I couldn't ever have learnt as a Nanny or at university. I knew the theory, and I soon learnt that went out of the window at three am when my own baby woke for the tenth time in pain from reflux, or when I had had some dairy by accident (my two youngest suffered with Cow's Milk Protein Allergy and reflux) and my baby was screaming in pain. I also learnt that when you aren't handing them over at the end of the day, being consistent is so much harder! Most of all it taught me compassion, exhaustion, love and to be absolutely non-judgemental. The families I helped sang my praises, and I was recommended across the globe.

Before the pandemic I worked one-to-one with families but this has changed. My approach was so popular I reached the ceiling of how many families could benefit from my expertise. So, I did something I had never done before and enrolled on my first ever business course. Since October 2020 I have completed four more courses, been to NYC on a business retreat, and as a result I now help over 25,000 parents daily. My CALM (Consistent, Achievable, Loving, Manageable) approach is well known in my community and my one hundred percent five star rating on Trustpilot shows that my approach still works, despite moving from one-to-one to one-to-many. I have launched nine online courses, run my signature sleep course nine times (so far), created a free to access sleep workshop, a community where parents can access my help for free and a paid-for membership. This book is a continuation of this desire to help as many parents as possible to sleep well.

I love showing parents that parenting doesn't need to be exhausting. More importantly, juggling work, life and a baby can be a pleasure. You can be a gentle parent, have a baby who sleeps well and who fits into your lifestyle – whatever that means to you.

Hannah x

Printed in Dunstable, United Kingdom

71066889R00120